A BEGINNER'S GUIDE TO
DRAWING

igloobooks

Published in 2014
by Igloo Books Ltd
Cottage Farm
Sywell
NN6 0BJ
www.igloobooks.com

CTP001 0514
4 6 8 10 9 7 5
ISBN 978-0-85780-533-1

Designed by HL Studios

Printed and manufactured in China

How to use this book

In the pages that follow we aim to take you through all the stages of drawing, whether it be still life, landscape, the living world or portraiture. We aim to show you how to choose your materials, how to study a subject or object, and how to decide where to put your first mark on the paper. We want you to learn how to carry a project through from start to finish, from that first mark to finished drawing, by using well tried and trusted processes. Most important of all, we want you to be confident in the decisions that you make.

In the Introduction you can become familiar with a variety of tools and materials to help you on your way, and you can practise using your pencils – a whole range of pencils if you wish, or just two or three if that seems right for you. You can make the marks that we've made, learn to draw a good circle, an ellipse, and other basic shapes.

Then you can begin to think about texture and tone. Hatching, cross-hatching, stippling, scribbling and using the side of the pencil will suddenly turn your marks on the page into a drawing. Your circle will become 3-D rather than flat on the page.

You can tackle the basics of drawing almost anything by following a step-by-step formula. Look at your object, note its basic shapes and put those basic shapes onto your paper. That's step one; we call that blocking in. Step two is to begin to improve the basic shape so that your outline is bolder and more complete. The third step is to add tone and texture, to make your drawing 'come alive'.

This format works for all aspects of drawing: objects that you see around the house, in the garden or at work, flowers, plants and animals or landscapes, both rural and urban. Those of us who are interested in producing a portrait of another human being can learn how to show the uniqueness of the person we want to portray, their physical individuality, as well as the distinctive personality of the subject.

It is not necessary to have had previous experience in drawing before tackling the exercises in this book. As a beginner we hope you will experience the excitement of depicting landscapes, still life and portraits.

Just remember, no one is born knowing how to draw. Each of us has to learn – by studying, thinking, and working. If you have the desire, you will surely learn too.

About the artist

David Carter, or just Carter as he is professionally known, was born and grew up in Cambridge, UK and knew that he wanted to draw from a very early age. He won many local drawing competitions, and excelled at art and technical drawing at secondary school. He graduated from a three-year course in illustration, with distinction, and immediately embarked on a professional career as a commercial artist.

Carter has over 20 years experience producing a varied range of artwork for the aerospace, automotive and pharmaceutical industries, educational projects, and even for wine producers. He has worked in the UK, Europe and Australia. He specialises in pencil drawing, pen and ink, watercolour, but is also adept with an airbrush, often mixing media to create exciting results. Indeed, combining pencil and watercolour wash was the technique he employed for one of his most interesting commissions – supplying all the drawings for the McLaren F1 supercar owner's handbook.

Although most of Carter's work is on traditional materials, he has also created artworks on motorcycle crash helmets and even scooter side-panels. When not working on commercial and private commissions, Carter is continually drawing and painting, and considers it vital to his own personal expression. His own preference is for drawing people, as he loves bringing someone's personality to life on the paper.

Carter now lives and works in Oxfordshire, UK with his artist partner and her two children. He has two cats, a dog, a rabbit and a classic car.

Introduction to drawing

How many times have you heard people say 'I'm the worst in the world when it comes to drawing', or 'I wish I could draw like that'. Well, why shouldn't you?

Most people who draw well or paint well learned to do so at school or college – very few people are born with these skills.

An artist or art teacher will say that learning the fundamentals of drawing is simply following instructions. You can learn how to draw a person, a bowl of fruit, or a landscape scene.

'But I draw like a child!' I hear you say. Well don't draw like a child anymore! Learn how to draw what you see.

This book deals with the basics of drawing. The exercises will become easier as you grow more confident and understand how to draw regular shapes and learn the principles of perspective. You'll find that with practice you'll soon begin to draw in a way that pleases you. And if it takes a bit longer than you expected, don't worry. Simply enjoy it!

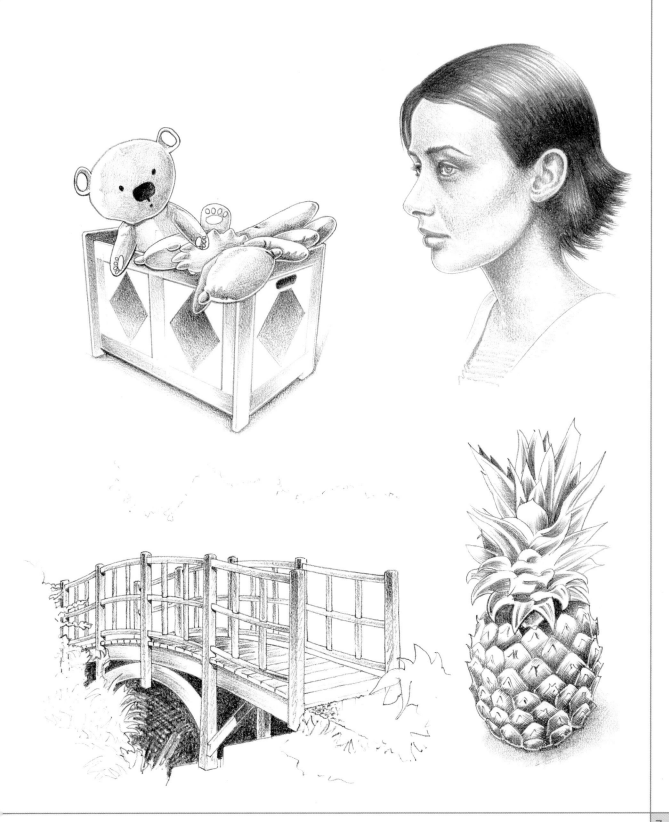

Tools to get you started

Once upon a time pencils were called 'lead' pencils. Nowadays, although we still talk about lead pencils, they're made of graphite, and graphite does the same job. However graphite is a form of carbon rather than lead.

There are around 20 grades of pencil, but you really don't need to buy all of them. They range from very fine, hard pencils of up to 9H to a soft, rather smudgy 9B. In the middle the range is 2H, H, F, HB, B 2B; an F pencil is similar to the standard HB, which is the pencil we can buy from the local stationery shop, but is perhaps a little more crisp.

Very fine pencils can be scratchy, whereas the extremely soft ones can easily smudge. To begin with you probably won't want to use anything too fine – maybe an H, F or HB – and then buy a small range of the softer pencils, perhaps a B, 2B, 4B and 6B. Remember that the higher the number next to the B, the softer and blacker the pencil marks.

Pencils may look alike, but they are actually very different!

The hardness of the core is often marked on the pencil – look for a number. The higher the number beside the 'H', the harder the writing core will be, and the higher the number beside the 'B', the blacker the writing core will be.

Pencils are relatively inexpensive, so it is worth buying a selection to see what suits you best.

Other essential materials

If you're drawing with pencil you need a pencil sharpener; you do need to have a good sharp point, particularly if you are drawing light lines for blocking in rough shapes or for putting delicate finishing touches to a work.

At some point in your drawing you will have to remove guidelines and rough blocking lines, so you will also need an eraser. Choose this piece of equipment carefully – some erasers are very hard and will damage the paper. Softer rubbers are better but they wear away quickly and leave a mess behind.

There is also the putty rubber (kneaded rubber), which will lift smudges or unwanted shading from your paper. To use a putty rubber you should hold it in your hand for a while. Within a few minutes the rubber will be pliable and you will be able to mould it as necessary. It can be moulded to a fine point for stippling, i.e. you can lift the pencil markings off a shaded area by using a dabbing technique, or you can fashion the rubber into a fine edge, and lift off whole lines of texture. Using a putty rubber in this way helps to avoid damage to the surface of the paper by rubbing with a hard eraser which can damage the surface of the paper and can even create a hole. It gets quite dirty with the pencil markings and you will have to cut off these blackened areas, or you can actually just pull them off and then knead the remainder into a good shape again.

Masking tape or low-tack paper tape will hold your drawing paper firmly to your drawing surface. This could be a drawing board, although it isn't necessary to spend a lot on such an item at this stage. Use the backing from a firm sketch pad.

Keep your drawing equipment together. Here are the basic items every artist needs: a selection of graphite pencils, some putty rubbers, a simple pencil sharpener, and some masking or low-tack tape to hold your drawing down.

Paper and drawing pads

You'll find that you're confronted by an enormous variety of paper types. Even cartridge paper comes in many weights and textures. Buy some economically priced cartridge paper for practising your marks and shapes. You might want a slightly higher quality for drawings you know you'll want to keep, but there is no need at this stage to buy expensive brands.

You will find that cartridge paper is easily damaged by too much rubbing out!

Extra-smooth drawing paper is good if you want to produce small, intricate studies, and it shouldn't suffer from a reasonable use of the rubber. It is, however, more expensive than cartridge paper.

Generally you won't need drawing pads for working at home as you'll find it easier to work on single sheets, but if you're intending to draw outside then you will benefit from having a pad that will fit into your bag.

There is a wide selection of papers available to suit all styles of drawing and painting. It may be useful to carry a small sketch pad so that you can draw wherever you go.

It is possible to spend a great deal of money on high quality art paper, but this is really not necessary for those new to drawing. If you want to preserve your drawings, it might be worth investing in some large folders so that you can store them flat, away from light or damp.

Setting up

It is recommended that you draw standing up; you will need an easel for this. But most people do actually prefer to sit at a table. Your table should be in a well-lit position near to a window. You will also need a lamp for extra light.

Sit comfortably in a position where you can easily look at your subject. If possible the bottom edge of your drawing board should rest on your knees and should lean against the table, and your subject should be directly in front of you at eye level. You should be concentrating on the subject rather than on your paper.

First of all, make sure you are holding your pencil correctly. Use a relaxed, open and flowing movement which if necessary utilises the whole arm. If you hold the pencil as if it were a pen, your drawing will probably be too small and there will be too much tension to allow free movement in your arm, wrist and hand. The most important point is that you are comfortable and can therefore enjoy the experience of drawing.

Artist's tip

It is really important that you are comfortable. If you prefer to stand, make sure your easel is adjusted so that you can draw comfortably. If you like to be seated, your chair must be the appropriate height as well. If necessary sit on a cushion, you may then need a foot stool as well.

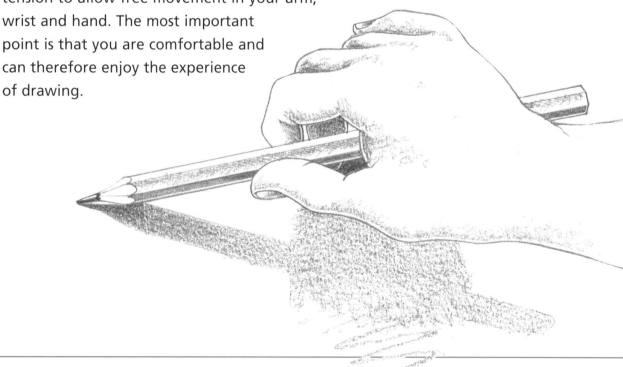

If you decide to use an easel, position it near to a window and also have good overhead lighting or a standard lamp.

Basic easels are inexpensive and can be found in a wide variety of stores, from specialist artists' shops to department stores. If you think that you would like to use it to produce landscape drawings outside, try to find a lightweight easel that will not weigh you down.

Techniques
Making marks

Now you've established your drawing area and bought some pencils and paper (and the all-important rubber), you're just about ready to begin making marks on your paper. It probably feels a bit like being a new child at school. However don't worry, think of your first attempts as a rehearsal. If they go wrong – start again. Now make some marks.

Draw a straight vertical line, then another. Now draw some horizontal lines and some diagonal lines. Now try drawing a square of straight lines, either vertical or horizontal, or both. Try to keep the distance between the lines equal and all the time keep them straight. Draw a square, and a triangle.

It's important to be able to draw shapes freehand because they're used all the time in drawings. As you'll see in the step-by-step section, a butterfly wing is based on the triangle, whereas cats and dogs are based on circular shapes.

So now draw a circle. Most people think they can't draw a circle but they can; just relax, hold your pencil as we saw earlier and draw. It doesn't matter if it's

a bit uneven, just draw another one, and continue drawing circles until your circle pleases you. You could try drawing a spiral as well.

Look at the examples opposite, and practise doing some of these marks on your paper. They're all marks that you can use for creating tone and texture, and we'll be talking more about that as well. For now just copy them and get used to the feel. Don't draw them too small – be flamboyant and create them large.

All good drawings are built up using basic marks, so it is worth taking the time to practise them. On the top row are straight lines, notice how they vary according to the pressure of the pencil.

In the next row are more circular, rounded and flowing shapes. Practice making continuous, even and curved lines. This is a vital skill when it comes to drawing circles and rounded shapes.

The third and fourth rows show various methods of shading which are used to add tone and depth to drawings. This is one area where using different grades of pencil can make a big difference, too.

Lines, hatching, cross-hatching

Basic shapes

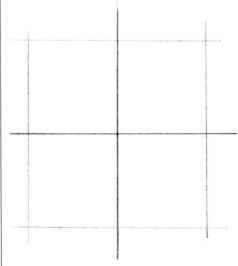

Fig. 1

We've already touched on drawing circles and other basic shapes as an aid to building up more complex images. Remember that some animals are based on a series of circles, such as a cat having a sulk, sitting upright with its back to you for example. Other animals are more box-like, and therefore their bodies are based on rectangles and their heads are squares.

Suppose, however, you wanted to draw a really precise circle – how might you go about that? Well, use a little bit of help.

Start with a square; find the central point (do this by drawing very faint diagonal lines) and then draw in a cross, You could use a ruler for all these lines; see Fig. 1.

Then draw your circle. You've had some practise now so perhaps you're more confident. The square should make it easier – see Fig. 2.

And now shade in one of the segments – see Fig. 3. The reason for this is to show that each segment is identical. If the segment you shaded is the same as the one to either the left or above, then you have drawn an accurate circle.

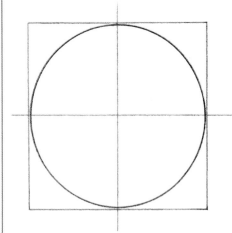

Fig. 2

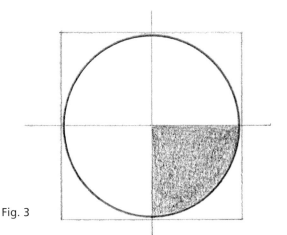

Fig. 3

Now try some freehand circles. Take a clean piece of paper, any number of different pencils and start to draw.

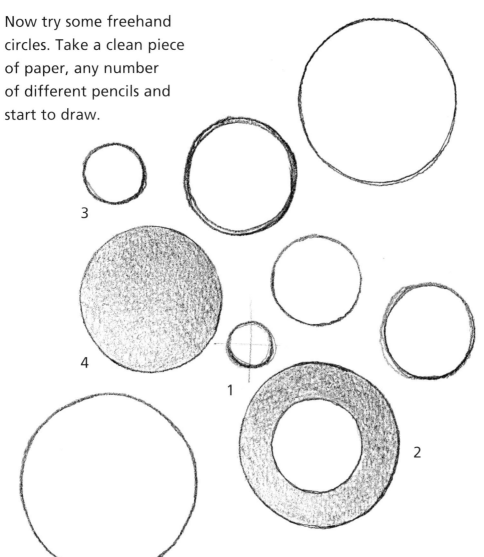

1. The very tiny circle has been drawn with guidelines, the centre of the circle is always a cross.

2. One circle has another circle within it, this is to practise parallel lines.

3. This circle has not worked very well, don't worry, move on to another one.

4. This circle has been given some texture, we'll talk more about this toward the end of this section.

Ellipses

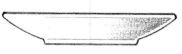

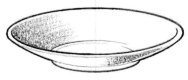

This plate at the top is being seen by you at eye level. It's rather like an architectural elevation and you see no part of the circle at all.

You are now looking at the plate from a different angle; what has actually happened is that you can see part of the inside of the plate. The shape now made by the rim is called an ellipse.

Lower the plate a little more and you can see most of the base of the plate, but you still cannot see the raised side nearest to you. The ellipse is now much deeper.

Now the plate is quite low, but what we're looking at here is not a complete circle. Look at the shaded edge of the plate, it's narrower nearer to you than it is on the other side. So the ellipse is now very deep.

Now you've lowered the plate so that you can look on it directly from above, a bird's eye view.
This is a full circle and the plate is completely flat. The shaded edge is the same thickness all around.

Drawing ellipses has to be learned, and drawing a freehand ellipse has to be practised. An ellipse is a continuous curve that has no angles and no straight edges.

The examples below show the incorrect versions, on the top row. The drawing on the left very obviously has angled corners – see Fig. 1. This one is exaggerated, but even a less obvious angle is incorrect. The drawing on the right is an attempt to avoid angled corners, but it's moved too far in the other direction and is again incorrect – see Fig. 2.

The drawing at the bottom has neither angles nor straight lines and it looks like an ellipse – see Fig. 3. Try drawing this yourself.

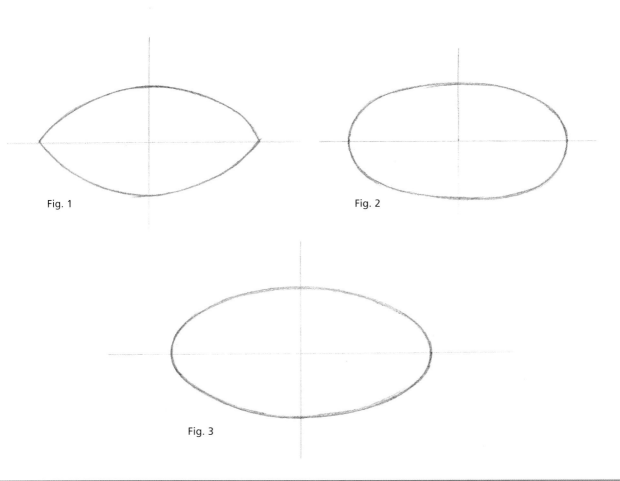

Fig. 1

Fig. 2

Fig. 3

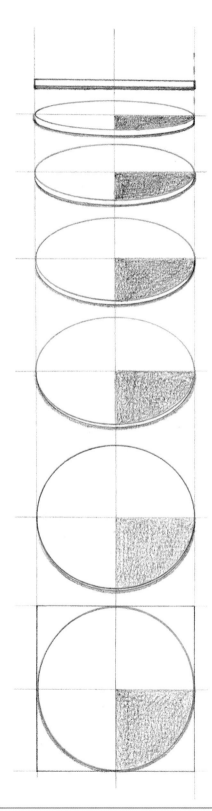

This exercise is similar to the previous one except that we're now looking at a disc rather than a plate. So the top drawing is very slim and flat.

Adding guidelines on your page just as we have will be really helpful.

The column here shows a circular object viewed from various levels. The object at the top is at eye level. It is a line or a horizontal disc and at the bottom it's a full circle. Put the full circle into a box, measure the sides of the box and exactly halfway, draw vertical and horizontal lines. If you wish you can also draw diagonal lines, they should all meet in the centre.

The second disc from the bottom is only slightly tilted and so your ellipse is very deep. Remember what the plate looked like when you were seeing it almost from above but not quite. Notice that the narrow edge is at this stage only a suggestion.

The third disc is more tilted. Have you noticed that you're now able to see the narrow edge?

As you move up the page the ellipses become narrower, remember to keep the shape correct at the sides, no pointed corners and no straight sides.

The shaded segment is one quarter of the ellipse. It should be an exact mirror image of the unshaded segments, in which case your ellipse is perfect. Shade in one segment of each ellipse, it should match the segment beside it as well as the one above. Drawing a freehand ellipse needs practise and confidence. You will manage to do this and you'll feel so thrilled when you've finished.

Practising ellipses

Balance a cylindrical object at an angle in front of you and start with a fresh sheet of paper. Make sure you're sitting so that you can easily see your object. Keep looking at the object as you draw.

Notice the overall shape, the height compared to the width. Are all of the edges curved or are they straight? Once you think you know the object well enough, that is the time to start your drawing. Always look at the tip of your pencil as you are drawing, that way you are in control of the pencil, and you are training your eye and your hand to work together. Always remember to draw what you see, not what you think you see.

Now change the position of your object and try again. You know the basic principles now, and practice is essential.

Take time every now and then to stop and look carefully at your drawing. If there are parts that you think are incorrect then redraw the lines that you think are wrong before you erase the others, it saves you just making the same mistakes again.

Remember that an ellipse can be seen at any angle – the wheel of a bus or a bicycle coming toward you or driving away. Now the ellipse is long and thin – quite different to those we've looked at so far. We could have looked at our plates vertically rather than horizontally, or we could have held them diagonally, and then the ellipse would have been diagonal. It really is just a question of how we observe them, and then drawing what we observe.

Cylindrical objects

Cylinders are solid figures that usually have a circular cross-section, as illustrated by the drawings of a tin of baked beans and a mug. Cylinders have gradual, evenly curving surfaces. You need to be able to show these curving surfaces in your drawing. Smooth progression of tone from light to dark creates an impression of a solid, rounded object. Adding a reflected light to the opposite side of the cylinder from the light source helps to create a 3-D effect.

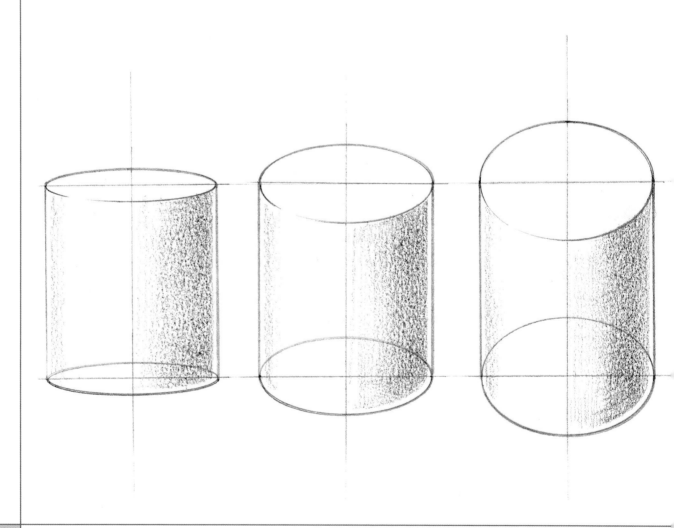

The images on these pages are of everyday objects. You've come a long way now from simply putting marks on the page!

The important point to remember now is that the ellipse at the bottom of the can must mirror of the ellipse at the top of the can, and the sides must be straight. Here you are working on a cylinder and ellipses. Start by drawing parallel lines and then draw in the ellipse top and bottom. When you think you have all the proportions right, erase the part of the bottom ellipse that is not seen.

As this is a metal object, the highlights will be quite strong, we'll talk about highlights and shading next.

Now do exactly the same with a mug. This is closer to you than the tin of beans and so the ellipse is deeper. Again, draw parallel lines and then draw in the ellipse top and bottom.

When you are happy with the shape add the handle. Take care with the position of the handle relative to the top and bottom, and notice that the width of the handle varies slightly because of the angle at which you're seeing it. Shading helps to give the mug a rounded effect.

This jug probably feels like an enormous step forward now because of the lip. To begin with forget that, and do exactly what you have done before – that is, draw the cylinder and the ellipses top and bottom. You will also be adding further ellipses for the pattern.

Now you're ready to add the details. Take care not to alter the shape of the bottom of the jug but gently round the edges, making sure they're exactly the same either side. To add the lip, draw what you see. Trusting your judgement is a big step forward and you'll find as you gain more confidence you will make well-judged marks. When you're happy that the lip is pointing in the right direction, add the handle.

You'll see three ellipses here; the top one belongs to the cup, the ellipses top and bottom of the flask are separate rims and the cylinder fits inside.

You might find it helpful to lightly pencil in the rough shape of the entire object so that you have the proportions in place. Then work on the main cylinder and the top and bottom ellipses. Now you're ready to tackle the upturned cup.

The flask also has a handle that fits neatly under the handle of the cup, and a strap. Again, draw what you see, keeping your eye on the pencil while you're making marks.

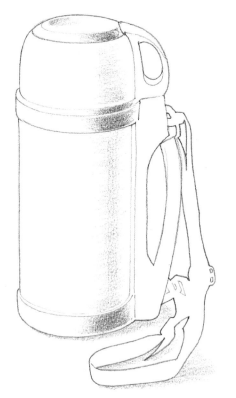

A watering can is a useful subject for practise. As the viewer you're looking down on this and the ellipse is very deep. So as usual – cylinder first, then add the ellipses. Then roughly draw in the two handles and the spout. Notice that the spout has straight lines but narrows as it reaches the rose (another ellipse). The bar supporting the spout forms a triangular shape. You'll find lots of geometric shapes appearing in your drawings, some people find it helpful to draw the triangle and build the objects around it. The handle at the top of the watering can is of uniform width, but you have to allow for seeing it from one side as it rises and then from the other as it falls. Look at the shape it makes inside the handle, it's pointed at the top. The side handle is also a uniform width – and is a good mixture of straight and curvy lines.

This object doesn't appear to be a true cylinder because it's wider at the top than it is at the bottom. But we know it is really of uniform width – we need to think about perspective. We will discuss perspective at the beginning of the Still life section. For now, unless you already know the rules of perspective, you could just draw what you see. There are plenty of artists who are self-taught and have never learned the rules of perspective.

Because the post box is so much larger than all of the other objects that we have dealt with so far, the effect of perspective is far more obvious. Not only do the vertical lines of the side of the post box converge towards the bottom, but the ellipses at the top and bottom differ greatly in shape because of your viewpoint to them. On the baked bean tin, the angle that your eyes needed to move up and down between the top and the bottom of the tin was very small. But the top of the post box is almost at eye level, whilst the bottom is on the ground, so your eyes have to move through a much greater angle up and down to view the complete object. This affects the angle of the ellipses. Those at the top are very thin, whilst the one at the base is much more open. Remember that despite their differing shapes all ellipses are just circles viewed from different angles.

Light source

While you are working on the texture remember to identify your light source – is your object lit from the back? If so, is the light source directly from the back or is it at an angle?

Look around your room. See how the light throws a shadow. How would you represent that shadow in a drawing? Certainly your shadow would be stronger close up to the object, and grow lighter until it fades away. Sometimes the shadows are very long, at other times they're shorter. It depends on the light source, how high or low it is.

Remember also to include the highlights, either by leaving your paper white and gently fading in your texture, or by removing the pencil marks with the putty rubber. You might find it easier to use both of these methods.

The drawing below gives an excellent indication of how the light source can enhance your drawing. The light is in the centre of the apple circle, so the area of the apple facing the light source is light and highlight. On the outside of the circle, however, the apples are in the shadow and so the highlights only appear where the light begins to catch the fruit. Notice how the shadow on the surface moves around with the angle of the shadow.

Textures

We've already looked at hatching, cross-hatching, using the side edge of the pencil and how the marks we put on the page grow into a drawing (see pages 16–17). Experiment with your pencils – you could stipple (using tiny dots) or even scribble.

These six apples are shaded and textured in a variety of ways. Let's examine the top row first.

The first apple, Fig. 1, is textured in a continuous tone. Use the side of a soft pencil and leave the paper white where you want your highlight to be. On the other side allow the tone to become quite dark.

The apple in the centre, Fig. 2, uses a scribbled effect. This really is just what it sounds like, a scribble or a doodle, going in all directions to form a texture. The scribble should become darker as you get into the darker shadow.

The next apple, Fig. 3, is textured by stippling. Put little tiny dots randomly all over the apple using a variety of pencils from HB to very soft. Use dark soft ones for the shaded area.

Remember to keep your pencils sharp when creating tone and texture, it's much easier to control what your pencil is doing if you have a good point.

The three apples at the bottom, Fig. 4–6, are drawn using hatching, cross-hatching and multi-hatching. This is another opportunity to acquire some practice.

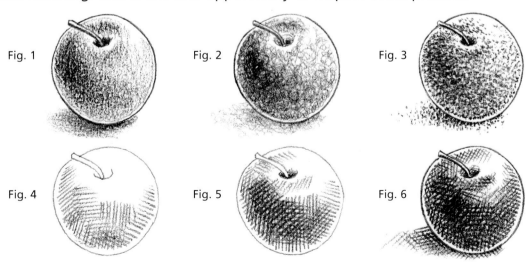

Fig. 1   Fig. 2   Fig. 3

Fig. 4   Fig. 5   Fig. 6

Using a viewfinder

A viewfinder on a camera is what a photographer looks through to compose a picture. For the artist, a viewfinder is a simple yet extremely useful painting tool which helps you to select a scene to get the best composition. So when you have decided what you intend to draw, a viewfinder can help you find the best view.

You can make your own viewfinder by taking a piece of light card, about A5 size or even smaller, draw a border inside the outer edges and then cut out the centre.

Or, if you find yourself painting outdoors and don't have your viewfinder, hold your hands together to form an opening, close one eye, and you will see a view. Move your hands around until the view is pleasing to you.

And why would you need one? Think about that holiday photo you have in a frame on your windowsill – the one with the mountains and the lake, and a church on an island in the middle of the lake. The island would make a nice photo as well.

It's the same with painting. The drawing opposite and the one below are actually part of much larger drawings elsewhere in this book. With the viewfinder the artist has, in effect, cropped out the rest of the drawing to focus on a particular area.

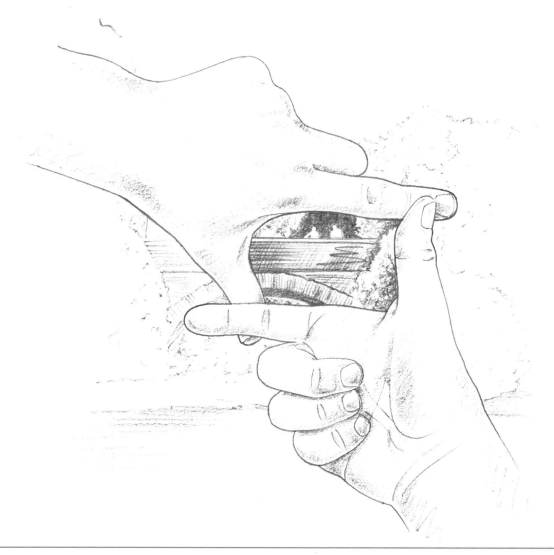

Enlargement with a grid

If you have a favourite photograph or picture that you would like to draw on a larger scale then consider using the grid method. Take care, though, not to spoil your original – take a photocopy first. This photo of a child with her kitten is a good example of how a grid can help you.

For instance, the child has beautiful hair that falls in natural waves. Although you could quite adequately draw the hair, it wouldn't necessarily look quite the same. You can be accurate in copying the way the child is holding the kitten, she's doing this very gently but the danger is that it might look as if she were strangling the poor creature.

So now it's time to mark up the photocopy – once you have decided how much larger to make your drawing. To mark up the copy with a one inch grid, use a ruler and start at the edge of one side and make a tiny mark for each inch. Do this around all sides and then complete the grid.

Now you must mark up your drawing paper. Perhaps you're marking up every two inches, thus giving you a 200% enlargement. Remember to keep the pencil lines very light because you'll need to erase them from the finished drawing later.

Now transfer the image in pencil, square by square.

Using a magnifying glass

You can use a magnifying glass to examine the object you are drawing more closely. This could have a two-way benefit:

● Looking at your drawing through a magnifying glass allows you to draw in fine detail
● You can examine more closely parts of the object you wish to draw

Move the object around rather than just concentrating on one part. Observe the whole appearance first and ask yourself if there is one part of this object that warrants special attention.

Once you have identified the most significant features, then decide what to draw. Keep looking back at your object while you are drawing. Use the magnifying glass to check the texture and tone. If you are using the glass to magnify the object you are drawing, make sure you hold it roughly the same distance from your object throughout your drawing so that the proportions stay true.

Still life

In the previous section we discovered a wide range of techniques showing how to draw a subject. In this Still Life section we will put these techniques into action.

To begin with we have chosen some fairly simple objects to study. Practising these will give you confidence and enable you to strengthen your ability.

Once you have had plenty of practice drawing real objects you find yourself noticing objects all around you, in your home and in the garden. In fact, just about everywhere. Look around you and you will find a painting just waiting to happen. You might be inspired by a toothbrush, a pile of shoes, or a collection of glassware.

If you're not inspired by your surroundings and are suffering from 'artist's block', why not look at the still life drawings of well known artists, such as Vincent van Gogh and his sunflowers, or Paul Cézanne and his wonderful fruit baskets. Copying is a good way to learn. And if you don't want to open the books and look at drawings by other people, then just pile the books up and draw them!

As time goes by, you will find that you gain an artistic perception of the world around you. You may begin to look at objects with new eyes, noticing the strong lines of their basic shapes and considering the composition and arrangement of items.

Simple perspective

One of the devices we can use to construct a good drawing is perspective. For some people the word conjures up horrors and they think 'I'll never be able to do that!' In fact it isn't so complicated. To understand this you need to follow a few rules:

- Any number of objects of the same size will look smaller the further away they are from you
- Objects appear less distinct the further away they are from you

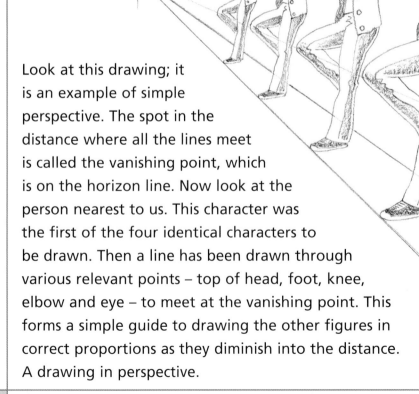

Look at this drawing; it is an example of simple perspective. The spot in the distance where all the lines meet is called the vanishing point, which is on the horizon line. Now look at the person nearest to us. This character was the first of the four identical characters to be drawn. Then a line has been drawn through various relevant points – top of head, foot, knee, elbow and eye – to meet at the vanishing point. This forms a simple guide to drawing the other figures in correct proportions as they diminish into the distance. A drawing in perspective.

The same rules have been applied to this drawing. Here we have a corridor, and the vanishing point is in the centre. Draw a vertical line from the top to the bottom of the page, making sure this passes through the vanishing point. Now draw a horizontal line across the page.

Now draw the nearest vertical line of wall on the corridor and an identical one on the opposite side, and the ceiling light and draw in all the guidelines to the vanishing point; from both sides of the light, and the top and bottom of the wall segment. It is now a simple matter of fitting in the other wall sections between the guidelines as they recede. Notice that the spaces between the wall sections become proportionately smaller as well. The same is true of the lights, they appear closer together the further away they are.

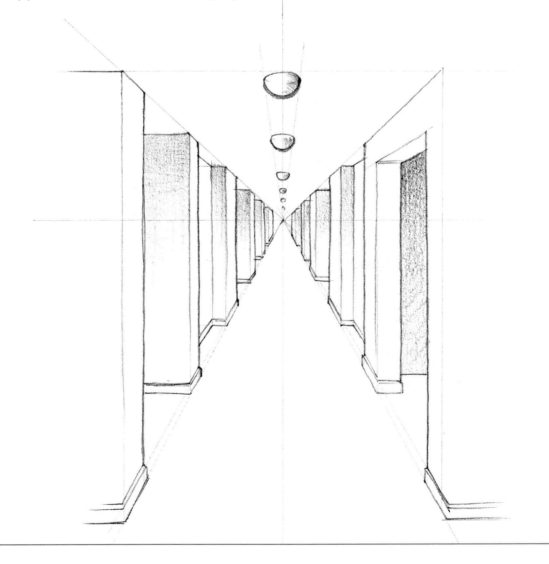

When you are drawing objects for the first time it's a good idea to build them gradually, taking care to create the basic outline. You can then go on to add tone and finally the finishing touches such as any blemishes or reflections to give your drawing that extra professional look.

The next few pages show how to go about drawing a variety of still life objects, starting with a banana.

1

It is important to make sure that the curve of the banana is just right before attempting any detail. You'll find it easier to get a good shape this way. Take care over the shape of the stalk and the flat end.

2

Outlined lightly yet precisely, the cross-section, or series of cross-sections, can be a useful aid in constructing a credible drawing. A banana has four or five irregular sides that give structure to a deceptively simple shape. Lightly sketching the cross-section can be useful to understand how the surfaces of the banana behave as it curves. Draw as many cross-sections as you feel you need. Here the banana actually has five sides.

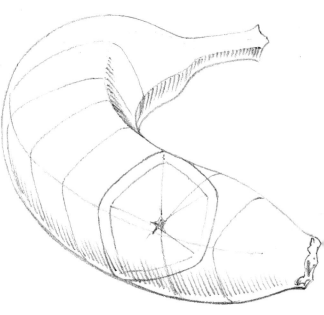

3

The final step is to add the tone and detail. Use the side of a soft pencil and make short strokes. Look at the shading beneath the stalk – see how it mirrors the shape of the banana. Notice the very neat shading which stops cleanly slightly away from the sides of the banana, thus accentuating the shape.

Now try using the same steps to draw a pear. It might look very simple on the page but appearances are deceptive. If you get your shape wrong at this stage you'll be disappointed with the finished result.

1

Take time in drawing the outline of this fruit. Does the pear stand upright? Most pears don't. So the first guideline to draw is the major axis, which will allow you to draw the simplified shape of the pear at the right angle. This particular pear is not sitting completely upright, so the major axis is drawn at a slight angle.

2

The pear is a very shapely fruit – make sure it has a sufficient curve. It's a good idea to put the stalk on at this stage before you add tone and texture. This way you'll be more aware of the final shape.

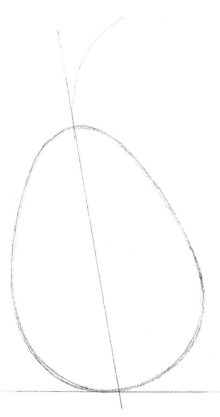

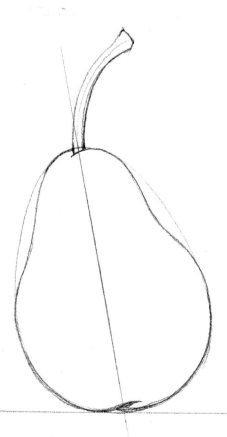

3

Now begin shading. Note where the
light shines, giving a highlight. Shade
the dark shadowy areas, building up
tone. Continue to build the tone up
over the whole shape, and lightly
bringing the tone up to the lighter
areas. Don't forget to put some
shadow beneath the pear – this helps
create the impression that the object is
standing on a surface.

Pineapples make a really interesting subject. The pineapple plant is a rosette of long fleshy pointed leaves and the fruit is surrounded by up to 200 individual fruitlets fused together. The fruitlets are arranged in two interlocking spirals, eight spirals in one direction, thirteen in the other. The fruit can be up to 12 inches long and weigh up to 10 pounds.

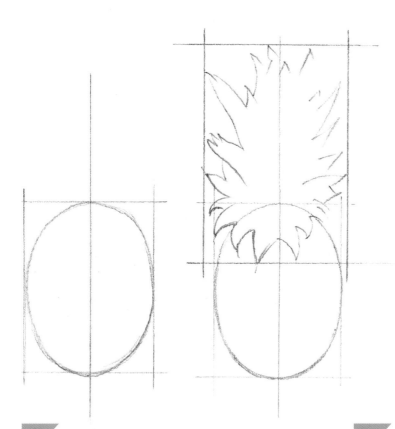

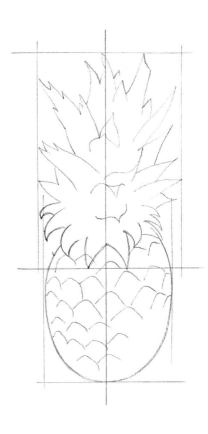

1

A pineapple has two very different parts, check the measurements here, you'll be surprised how large the leaf section is. Make sure your leaves are overlapping the fruit.

2

Gradually add the detail – there are lots of segments and leaves and you will need to put each one into your drawing at this stage. Once you are happy with the outline shape and proportions of the body and leaves of the pineapple, you can start filling in some more of the details, as in step three.

3

Now you're ready to complete the shapes, adding texture and tone to each one. The shape of the individual 'fruitlets' of the pineapple can be accentuated by adjusting the angle of your cross-hatching to match their angle. Now add the shading to the leaves. Don't forget to add some shading to the flat surface beneath the fruit.

After arranging the flowers in a vase, try to look at the flowers and understand how they are all made of simple shapes. At first, the arrangement may seem very complicated, but focus on just one flower and break it down. In the case of the daffodils, they have six almost diamond-shaped petals arranged around the base of the trumpet, which is just a truncated cone.

1

Although the top of the vase will be hidden in this drawing, it is important to know the size of the vase. And even though it is hidden, it's tidy to have the ellipse looking right, as well as good practice. To help you draw the trumpets, first try to identify in which direction the flowers are pointing, and then draw a line to represent the major axis. You can then draw the trumpets in the right direction and the ellipses at the right angle.

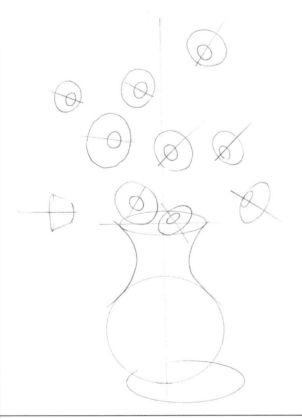

2

At this stage it's a good idea to have all of the flower heads in place. You can tell from looking at flowers in a vase that sometimes they could be better arranged. It's the same with your drawing. Sometimes it's good to have a space, sometimes it isn't. Take plenty of time now making sure that your arrangement is just as you want it. Think also about the flowers pointing in all directions – daffodils are so interesting in profile.

3

The shading on daffodils is very subtle.

The traditional daffodil has a golden yellow colour all over, but the trumpet may often feature a contrasting colour. The inside of the trumpet is heavily shaded – use a very soft pencil for this. The petals are gently shaded with hatching but the petals' edges have highlights.

Finally, don't forget to highlight the vase and put its shadow on the flat surface.

Still life objects have moved on now that we're in the 21st century. We are surrounded by modern technology and there is absolutely no reason why these objects shouldn't form part of our portfolio, in addition to fruit and scenes of domesticity.

1

The general outline of this mobile phone looks simple, but be aware of the perspective. The lid of the phone needs to be at an angle. At this first stage of blocking in the basic shape you should ensure that all your lines are parallel.

2

Now you can add the main shapes. Keep the lines as clean as possible and don't add any shading until you are perfectly satisfied that the phone has all the curves in the correct places. Notice how you can now see depth in the object.

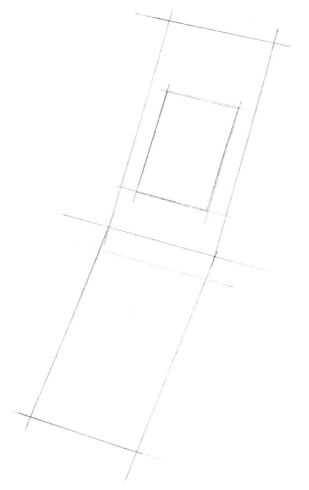

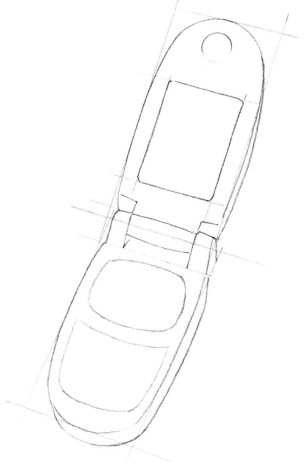

3

Now you can add the texture. Remember to include shading below your phone – this shows the surface. Notice the very dark shading between the lid and the main section of the phone which depth to this area. You can really enjoy experimenting with the shading on this object. Hatching and cross-hatching at different angles will help to show depth. Plenty of highlights will give the viewer a more convincing notion that this is a shiny object. Notice that the very fine details, such as the numbers on the key pad, are only roughly sketched. This does not detract from the image in any way.

Portable radio/CD players come in a variety of shapes. This one is a mass of curves, rounded edges, buttons, circles and ellipses. This is a perfect opportunity to practise the shapes we've been looking at over the previous pages.

1

Place your object at a slight angle to make the drawing more interesting. The parallel lines will keep your drawing in an accurate perspective. This will also give you practice with ellipses and foreshortening. Outline the general shape with an HB or H pencil.

2

Now sketch in the shapes that you see. It's important to show the depth of the machine at this point – it has quite a chubby shape, you do have to fit in quite a number of buttons and circles and you need to feel happy with these before starting to add texture and tone.

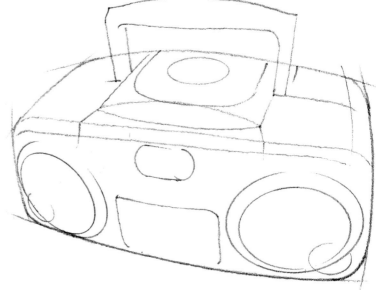

3

You will need to keep some light areas on this drawing to suggest
the metallic surface, but use light shading as it should not look
too shiny. You might want to use your putty rubber to remove
the shading – this helps to suggest reflections, particularly on the
handle. Notice the hollow section inside the handle; the shading
there is very dark to give depth. The speakers on the front of the
machine also need to show depth so use a variety of textures such
as single hatching and cross-hatching to differentiate.

Toys are popular objects to draw. Although there are very simple lines in this first drawing, it is actually quite a complicated structure. Remember to include the guidelines so that you can manage the perspective accurately.

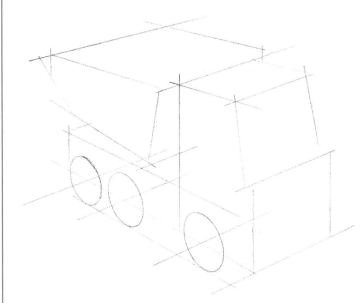

1

Put in the bare minimum number of lines at this stage. Obviously you need the three wheels and the cab, and also the tip-up. Remember to draw your guidelines in so that you can line the wheels up correctly.

2

Don't bother with shading yet. Now you can put in all of the extra lines. Notice the ellipse on the wheels – it changes as the wheels move further away. Keep the edges rounded, so there aren't any sharp angles.

3

Now that your second stage is complete you can start
to add tone and texture. First of all see where your light
source is and study the shadow. As this is a toy for a young
child the edges are rounded and quite smooth. Pick out the
highlights on the wheels and lift any excess shading from
the hub caps, that will help to make them look metallic.

When you're out with your sketch book in your bag, why not stop on occasions and draw a large object such as a car. Of course, you can't guarantee that it won't be driven away before you've finished your drawing. The car drawn here is another very rounded object.

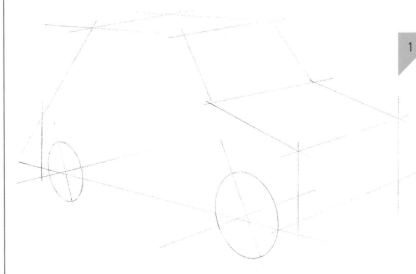

1

Aim to put in just the very basic shape. Consider the angle of the car and the appropriate perspective. Notice how simply you can suggest the shape of the bonnet and windscreen.

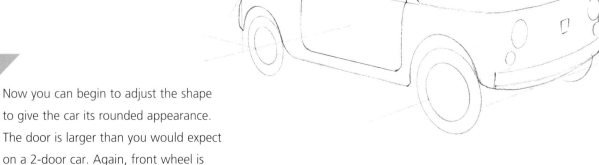

2

Now you can begin to adjust the shape to give the car its rounded appearance. The door is larger than you would expect on a 2-door car. Again, front wheel is very much larger than the back wheel.

Artist's tip

If cars are your thing, take time to draw different models. Vintage cars in particular incorporate beautiful details; they offer the artist a host of opportunities and look great as pencil drawings.

3

The interior of the car has quite heavy shading, which you would expect. The exaggerated shading on this car is also to be expected, because we need to know that it is so shiny, particularly on the bonnet.

Detailed features

With practice you will start to become aware of minute detail on objects around you that is hardly visible at first glance. Use a magnifying glass to examine the object you are drawing more closely. You can also enlarge your own work as it progresses so that the more intricate parts of your drawing are easier to see.

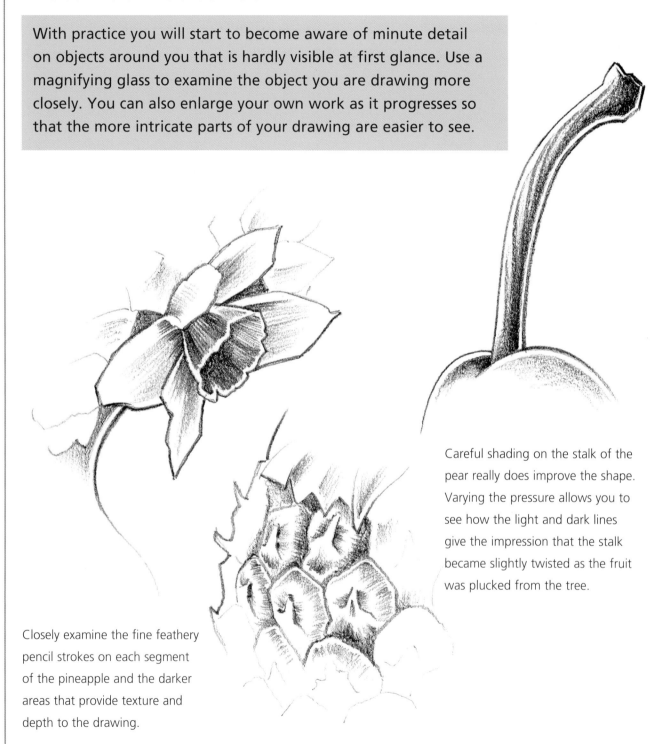

Careful shading on the stalk of the pear really does improve the shape. Varying the pressure allows you to see how the light and dark lines give the impression that the stalk became slightly twisted as the fruit was plucked from the tree.

Closely examine the fine feathery pencil strokes on each segment of the pineapple and the darker areas that provide texture and depth to the drawing.

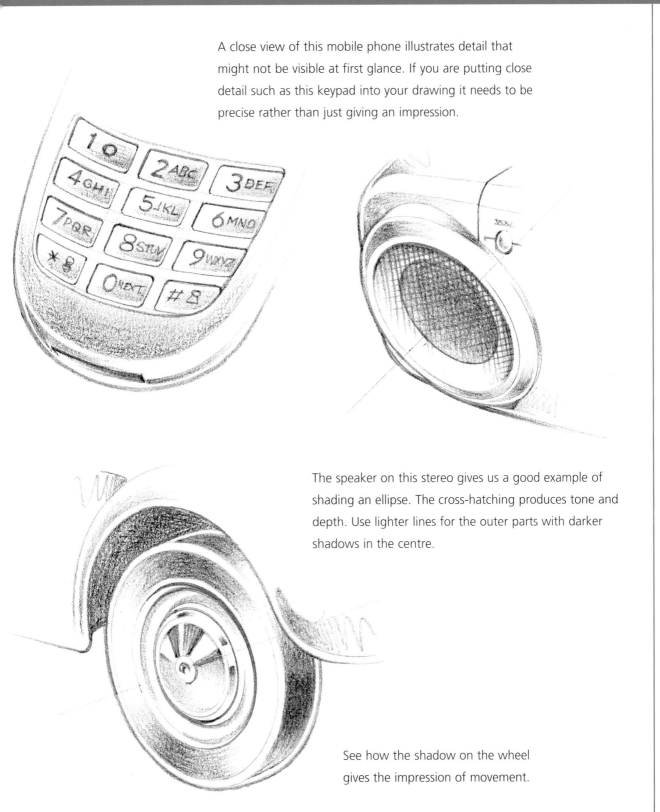

A close view of this mobile phone illustrates detail that might not be visible at first glance. If you are putting close detail such as this keypad into your drawing it needs to be precise rather than just giving an impression.

The speaker on this stereo gives us a good example of shading an ellipse. The cross-hatching produces tone and depth. Use lighter lines for the outer parts with darker shadows in the centre.

See how the shadow on the wheel gives the impression of movement.

Composition

Any group of objects can create an interesting picture. When we think of still life composition, we immediately think of bowls of fruit, or flowers, in particular Vincent van Gogh's sunflowers.

We often see still life drawings of the potting shed. Why not look at the inside of your garage? Tools make a good subject, for instance, it can be quite challenging to portray shiny objects.

It is probably a bad idea, however, to mix unrelated objects in a drawing unless there is a particular reason for it.

Once you've made your decision it is important to think about arrangement. Your drawing will have a more pleasing appearance if your objects are touching or overlapping. Think about adding height to your group or pile of objects.

The building blocks are favourites with artists – they give good practice at drawing a cube, but of course they are all placed at different angles. This is where perspective is important.

Always be aware of the space between objects. Sometimes the space is as important as the object itself, because if the space is incorrectly portrayed, then you won't be satisfied with your work.

These items of glassware
make a lovely drawing.
Notice the ellipses in the
base of the decanter and
the glass and at the tops –
there are so many.

The highlights here really
do exhibit the impression
of glass.

Still life objects can be almost anything that interests you. Here, three nuts and bolts are arranged in an interesting group.

Earlier we looked at drawing cylinders and this should be your starting point. You have three cylinders here – don't worry about putting the spirals in yet.

Now add the nuts, and remember that any nut that touches the surface will be resting on a flat edge. The nuts are hexagonal, and you will only ever see three of the six flat sides, although you will see the shape of two other facets from the top. The sixth will be hidden behind the bolt.

To draw the nut you might think of it as another cylindrical shape. Notice how one edge of the nut appears to be curved and that curve is mirrored on the opposite edge as it goes behind the bolt. When you have that basic shape drawn in, add the angled edges (you can actually see four of them on each nut). Make sure you include the bevelled edges to give a realistic finish. Now is the time to put the spirals onto the bolt. Keep a really constant curve and remember the ellipses at the end of each bolt.

Finally, we come to the shading. Identify your light source and notice that, as well as the highlight from the light, there is also a reflected light which will bounce of any light surface.

Chilli peppers are a beautiful shape and pile on top of one another in a pleasing way. Notice how the two peppers which are on the surface sit beside one another. They aren't overlapping but because of the rounded form of the chilli you should make sure that it doesn't appear flat. It is essential to have the positioning correct for it to be a credible drawing.

The skins of chillies can often be very shiny, and can display some interesting reflections and highlights. Although this is a pencil drawing it would seem that the chilli on top of the others is a different colour. The texture is darker (from using a softer pencil) and the highlighting stronger.

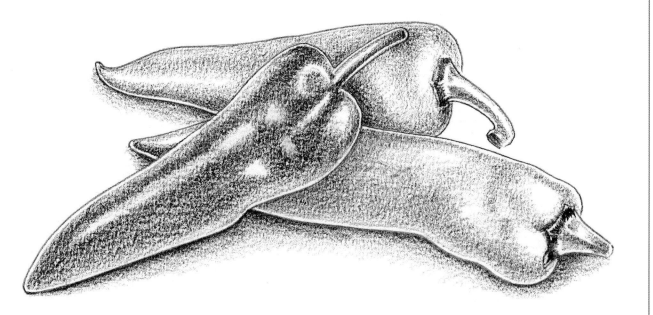

Objects in a setting

The objects we see every day can be arranged in all kinds of different ways to create pleasing compositions. This study of a collection of common schoolroom objects, reminds us of classic still life paintings by artists such as Vincent van Gogh and Cézanne. Look at the placement of the book, ruler, pencil and apple.

To begin your drawing, you might start with a few lines and an ellipse to show the horizon line and general shape of the objects. Now draw in the outlines, beginning with the largest and most complex object, the book. Leave out the shading for the time being. Once you are satisfied you have a good outline, examine the effects of the strong light source, which creates sharp contrasts.

The spine of the book and the part of the table that is underneath the open cover and pages are almost black, whilst the shadows of both the book and the apple become lighter the further they are from the light source. Notice also that the shadow of the ruler is curved on the right-hand page of the book and broken in the place where the left side of the book meets the surface of the table.

Plums, grapes, bananas and apples in a bowl – this is a typical still life drawing. We are looking at this subject from above and so we can see deep into the bowl. Have you noticed the tiny tip of a banana at the front of the bowl, between the centre apple and the one to its left? That sort of detail presents a natural look to the drawing and a pleasing result.

Another area that catches the eye is the area with the bunch of grapes where we see the stalks. It would have been so easy to add another grape here. Of course we all know that the stalks are there but we might not necessarily think to include them in our drawing. Always look for that extra small piece of interest to make your drawing special.

Remember to find the light source and add shading and reflection – most fruits have beautiful shiny skins and you can, with practice, manage to make them shine.

Bananas are such a joy to draw, and unpeeled they are even more interesting. Notice the shadow where the banana peel has been folded back; you need to create shadow on the edges because the light is shining from the left. And don't forget to keep the top of the banana in your drawing – they're always there on a peeled banana because, of course, that's how we open them!

Remember we noticed earlier that a pear rarely stands upright, here's another that is leaning. This one is delicately textured where the light is bouncing from it.

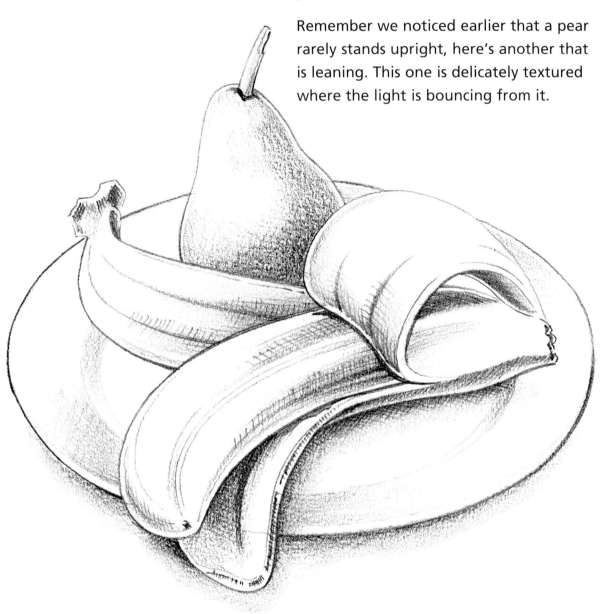

This basket of bread rolls provides an excellent opportunity to study contrasting textures, as well as lines and shapes. Begin your study by drawing in the largest and simplest shape, the form of the basket. Then sketch in the various smaller shapes – ellipses, circles, semi-circles – of the different kinds of bread. Notice the numerous lines and gentle curves created by the round basket and intertwined reeds.

Here is a collection of very chunky glassware. These are very different from the stylish glassware we studied earlier. They may not be elegant but the many facets make for interesting reflections and shapes.

One important point to remember is that the two glasses on the right are identical. Therefore your drawing of these two, in particular, needs to be identical as well, except for the angle. Notice the ellipse on each of these objects – they are all different because they aren't standing in a straight line.

Once you've worked out what's actually in front of you, you're ready to make an initial drawing of the simple shapes you see. Draw the outlines of the shoes, including the lines made by various features such as soles and laces. You will notice that there are at least four different types of lace, some of them flat, some round and of varying thicknesses. When you are satisfied you have a good outline, turn your attention to effects of shading. Begin with larger blocks suggesting dark or bright colours such as the stripes and patches on the trainers and the shading on the dark casuals.

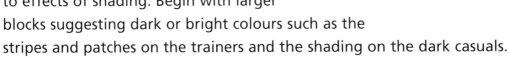

When we look at this toy box we can see lots of contrasting shapes. The box itself contains mostly straight lines that form rectangles and squares, while the toys peeping out from inside it suggest softness through their round curves, and also a certain disorder. Now try a more thorough outline, starting with the box and then moving to the large teddy bear. Notice all the arms and legs – can you tell which toy each of them belongs to, or do some belong to toys that are hidden inside the box? It's important to work all of this out because it will make a difference once you start adding detail and shading.

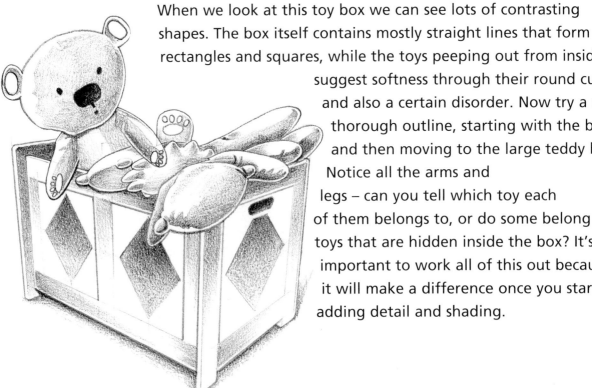

This drawing is a perfect example of something we might see quite often but never really look at. And of course we are seeing it from a different angle. Normally we're either in the car wash itself or we're driving into it.

Parts of the drawing are quite indistinct. The powerful water jets are causing spray and so there is little clarity around the back end of the car. Don't be afraid to leave these areas rather vague – remember you should draw only what you see. For instance you can actually only see one wheel clearly.

The windscreen, which is being pounded by the water, would normally be quite dark inside the car wash but the water is creating clouds of misty spray. You'll need to either leave the paper white or remove the texture with your putty rubber, but you will also need to allow the misty areas to appear gradually so use a stippling effect to make sure there are no hard lines.

Living world

The living world section generally covers animals and plants. That's an enormous range of subjects but one that is very popular with artists. Wouldn't we all just love to be able to draw our cat or dog?

Until now we've been looking at ways of drawing objects that are stationary. We will still be doing that in this section with, for example, plants in the garden or in pots. But we will also be thinking about how to draw animals, maybe our own pets and as we know it's difficult enough to manage a photograph of a pet, let alone a drawing.

To draw birds, squirrels, fish or shrews you'll need to consider looking at magazines or books, or even on the internet. You can find shrubs and flowers in books and magazines also, but you might like to try drawing these in your own garden. If you haven't already tried some drawing outside this might be just the right time to start.

It's perfectly fine to copy, in fact we've already looked, in the introduction at how to make a grid and copy a favourite picture. Taking photographs of pets or animals that don't move very quickly is an excellent idea because you can print your photo at the size you want.

You might even take a photo of swans and their cygnets and draw a picture like the one opposite.

Drawing animals

When drawing any animal you should be thinking about its most important features. You're now drawing a living creature – even if you've copied it from a book or a photograph, your drawing needs to look as if it's living.

Constructing the shape correctly is the first step, after all you don't want it looking like a badly stuffed toy. Draw your first outline carefully and decide where the eyes should be and then the ears. Ears are really important with animals because we can, after all, recognise many animals by their ears, something that is not true of humans.

Finally, the tail – make sure this appears from the right part of the body – too high or too low and the drawing loses its credibility.

On these pages you will be able to see the preparatory studies for this beautiful creature. Notice how full of life the tail is, and how the squirrel is peering around to make sure that it is safe while enjoying the food.

1

You need to make the outline of the animal very accurate at this stage. Squirrels have amazingly supple bodies. They stretch themselves long and thin and then they look quite delicate. They can also huddle themselves into very rounded forms. Place the ears very roughly but also very carefully so that they sit in just the right place on the head, and then place the eye. Make sure it's large enough – a squirrel's eye is larger than you think.

2

Now add more of the facial details and identify where the creature bends. Make sure that the feet are large enough to balance the squirrel – notice the perspective here. The foot nearest to us looks shorter because it's pointing toward us, whereas the other foot is pointing away so seems to be longer.

3

Now you can add the fur. Use a very soft pencil for the squirrel's fur, probably a 5B, and put plenty of shading where his body is folded over above the thigh. Remember to leave some white fur on the front of the body and on the thighs. The most exciting bit to draw is obviously the tail – see how the hairs separate and appear really bushy yet still look so soft.

Four-legged animals tend to follow a common shape, so whether you're drawing a lamb, a dog or a horse, the general shape for the first stage of your drawing is pretty standard. Generally speaking, they move in similar ways as well. Remember that generally, cats have quite short legs compared to dogs. If, however, your chosen drawing is a long-haired cat or a Scottish terrier, the legs will be very short.

1

This is an example of the common shape of four-legged animals. See how the circles and guidelines simplify the initial drawing. This cat to the right is turning to look at something so there is a variation here. This way we have the opportunity to work on a cat's face.

2

Now it's time to add a little more detail. It's very important to find the right position for the face. It looks far too simple in this drawing, but if the features aren't correctly positioned you'll find the end result, when the cat has its fur in place, isn't so pleasing. Although you'll be able to rub out the offending details and start again, getting it right at this stage is so much more satisfying.

Artist's tip

It's a good idea to study skeletons of animals – this way you'll be more aware of their joints and what they really look like under their coats. Animals' coats are, however, very different. Even the coats of dogs and cats vary enormously and there's no other way but to practise to find the best way to show off your skills.

3

Now we have a finished cat. Notice the careful attention to the eyes – this cat thinks there was a movement somewhere that could indicate a meal is close by. The highlight in the eye is most important – this gives it the expression.

Now you can start adding texture to suggest thick fur. The pencil strokes should all go in the direction that the fur grows. This cat has very dense, short fur. You'll find that all cats have very short fur on the nose. You could use stipple here to indicate very short fur, and add some highlight. When you draw in the whiskers ensure the lines are straight – draw it in one quick movement.

Here we have another example of using the familiar four-legged animal shape, in this case the particularly square shape of the English bull terrier. This time the animal is not in profile, but is a more 3-D shape, standing at an angle, but looking directly at us.

1

Circles are again used to help simplify the dog's shape below. A larger circle for the chest area and a smaller circle for the rear instantly help us achieve the correct proportions. As with the cat, take care with the length and the placement of the legs in proportion to the body. A central line, at the correct angle, helps position the head. Care needs to be given to the angles as well as the shape of the head. The tail at this stage need only be a single line, but is carefully drawn to enhance the typical attitude of this breed.

2

Once we are satisfied that the basic sketch gives us a satisfactory characteristic image of the animal, we can add detail. The tail is now drawn – thick at the base and tapering to the end, but following the original angle. The eyes are the most important feature in any face and need to be carefully indicated, round circles are sufficient at this stage. The nose can be added now and the feet more defined.

3

Our bull terrier now becomes life-like. It has an extremely short, dense coat. Therefore the surface is defined by the muscular configuration beneath the skin, thus fleshing out the skeletal shape. Now assess the direction of the light source and gently fill in the areas of shade, remembering that less light penetrates inside the ears, so add deeper tones there. The eyes need careful detailing, and highlighting gives them life. Leave areas of the surface blank or using a putty rubber to suggest a strong, muscular animal with a shiny coat.

We now transfer the same technique to an animal of a totally different shape, based on a triangle. A cockerel is in profile looking straight ahead, probably about to peck at a seed of corn he has spotted on the ground.

1

The largest circle gives us the puffed out chest. Two angled lines from the centre of the circle give us his strutting stance and show where to place that small circle for his head, with another large circle for his splendid tail feathers. The exaggerated outline of the comb makes the head appear even smaller, and the position of the drooping wing is indicated.

A third line completes his triangular shape and the angle of his back. The line from the head to the large central circle then continues to the tail and gives a satisfactory impression of a cockerel in characteristic pose.

2

Now add detail to the outline. The comb on the head becomes more deeply indented, and the beak and wattle are sketched in. The feathers should only be indicated in outline at this stage, although the layers down to the wing and the feet can be suggested.

3

Now is the moment to enjoy adding the detail of the cockerel's plumage. As with the drawing of the fur of animals, we need to rely on the contrast of light and shade and use strokes of different lengths and density. The individual tail feathers should be placed carefully in relation to each other. Each plume has a central rib with individual hairs growing from it. The feathers fall in layers. The underneath feathers should be more darkly and densely shaded – make sure the lines all go in the same direction. The upper feathers of the tail and the large feathers falling over the back and side need to be left lighter in tone so that they are in contrast.

Using contrasting lengths of pencil strokes we can indicate different textures on all parts of the cockerel's shape. The upper feathers of the wing require curved, elongated lines and under his chest short strokes are used. Overall the pencil strokes must mimic the direction of growth.

His legs and feet are detailed and a suggestion of grass completes the illustration.

We now tackle a creature that is a completely new shape, but we continue to use the now familiar technique of simplifying the overall outline – this time into geometric shapes. The wings are based on triangles.

1

In this view of the butterfly only three of the wings are visible, and are simplified into three triangular shapes – in fact they're rather like sails. We need to place them carefully in relation to each other. As with the other animals, this is the most important stage to ensure an accurate finished drawing.

2

To give more definition to the outline, you can draw in the scalloped outer edge of the wings. Emphasise the thicker front edge and add the delicate antennae and the proboscis (this is the little snout-like nose). The butterfly begins to take shape.

3

Observe the pattern on each wing. Using long pencil strokes, continue to outline the edges and then the linear segments on each of the forewings. The contrast of light areas and dark patches, using short dark strokes closely drawn indicate the beautiful wing pattern. The individual markings on the hindwings are simply drawn, but still suggest the complicated detail. The outline of the body is diffused by the use of short gentle lines to suggest hair. The delicate antennae are lightly drawn and the foliage needs only to be suggested.

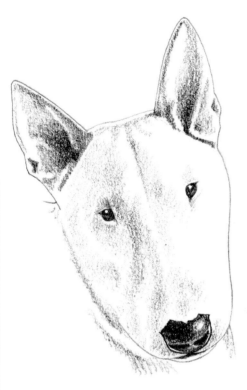

Detailed features

We looked at detail earlier, in particular the use of a magnifying glass. The details on this page, however, aren't intricate lines that require a magnifying glass, but are simply enlarged versions of the drawings we've already seen over the last few pages. A good drawing will still look good when seen on a larger scale.

We notice in the enlarged version of the bull terrier's head, just how small the eyes are. But they still have expression and you can almost hear this animal asking to be stroked or to go for a walk, it has a pleading gaze. Note that the nose has strong central areas of shading with a carefully placed highlight. The eyes have a triangular outline that gives them the characteristic expression.

The detail of the front paw clearly shows the toenails. Very often people fudge the feet of animals (or even people) and just give an indication that they exist – with animals they can be hidden in grass or behind rocks. The feet are sometimes difficult but you need to persevere and then you'll find you can produce a satisfactory piece of work.

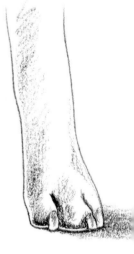

The pupils in the eyes of a cat change shape and this cat at present has vertical ellipses, probably because it's outside (looking for the mouse or shrew it thinks it has seen in the grass). You also get a better look at the whiskers and can see how smoothly they curve.

These are all parts of the animal drawings we've seen on the preceding pages. The cockerel and the butterfly couldn't really be more different. The magnified selections from these two creatures show some interesting facts that we might have missed when looking at the original drawings.

This part of the butterfly drawing, the head, antennae and the nose and mouth, appear very furry indeed when magnified so much.

On the full drawing of the butterfly this wing is underneath the others and although it can be clearly seen, it isn't as obvious and our eye is drawn to the forewings. The wings are made up of a fine epidermal membrane that spans the spaces between a network of wing veins that fan out into the wing shape. On this drawing you can just about see where the veins are. The patterns are marvellously elaborate.

The fleshy crest on this bird's head is called a comb; usually, but not always, it grows larger and is more prominent on the cockerel than on his female counterpart. Its purpose is to aid cooling. The same applies to the wattle, the fleshy, wrinkled fold of hanging skin under the beak. The wattle has no feathers and so to distinguish this fact the area should be left very lightly textured, perhaps with very light stippling.

The beak is small – this may be because male and female chicks have their beaks trimmed.

This detail of the cockerel's plumage is taken from the wing pad just above the legs. The feathers here are quite long and on this close-up you are able to see the veins of some feathers and also distinguish the very fine barbs that protrude from the veins.

Gallery

Cast your mind back to the pages where we looked at drawing animals, in particular the blocking in of first steps (pages 68–76). Now look at the cat lying in the front of this domestic scene. Draw a large circle for the body and a small circle for the head.

The dog should have a large circle for the hip area and the head, and an enormous circle for the chest (this will incorporate the head circle).

Once you're happy that all is in place you can begin to add more detail. You will notice that the dog's body twists. Animals have the ability to twist their bodies into shapes which

seem almost impossible, for instance a cat can lie comfortably sleeping in incredibly contorted positions.

One of the points you need to bring out in this drawing is the difference in the animals' coats. The cat is soft and has what we would call a sleek coat – we can express this through highlighting, it should look quite shiny. The dog is also shiny, but its coat is short and more stubbly.

Both animals appear to be looking at us. Make sure that you don't draw the eyes too large and that you highlight them, otherwise they will look unfinished. The dog's eyes look rather more friendly than those of the cat – cats are often more guarded.

Imagine you were just starting this drawing. Your first step would be to find the centre line. This owl has turned its head slightly, and the angle at which we are seeing it causes the body to be rather like an oval at an angle. Make sure that your central line balances the bird well, so that it is able to stand without falling over.

Place a circle for the head at the top of the oval, and lightly mark in the ears. The eyes line up with the inside of the ears. The beak is quite large.

The feathers on the front of the owl are roughly drawn but the wing feathers are darker and more strongly textured. We get the notion of layer upon layer of tiny feathers and we just know that this bird would be so soft were we able to touch it. This softness contrasts with the strong hard claw and the beak which both look rather dangerous.

The owl's eyes are stern and all-knowing and reinforce the image we have of the wise owl. Finally, add texture to the ears.

At first glance we might think this is just a fish in a bowl, but look harder, the bowl is actually not spherical but is flat at the front and back. The bowl is at a slight angle, so on the left hand side we are looking at the outside of the curved edge. On the right hand side of the drawing we can see the curved edge through the glass.

When drawing anything made of glass, it's worth thinking first about the external shape of the object itself – maybe imagine what the object would look like if it were opaque instead of transparent. In the case of the goldfish bowl, the actual shape is quite simple, but appears more complex because you can see through it, and the water refracts the light differently to the air space at the top. As before, just draw what you see, and try to concentrate on what you are actually looking at – whether it's the side, or the back, or the bottom of the bowl.

The fish should be a little easier, as it's a relatively simple shape. But, in the case of this ornamental goldfish, its long flowing tail makes it a little more interesting. We are seeing it swimming toward us so the foreshortening effect means we don't really know its size. The dorsal fin appears very large and its pectoral fins quite small.

The overall impression in this drawing is of movement. Look at the instability of the animal – if it were not moving very quickly it would obviously fall over. We are also aware of movement by the flying hair of the tail and the mane. At least three of the feet are off the ground and the fourth appears to be kicking up dust.

Despite the twisted contorted body shape, it still very clearly portrays the form of a horse. The very muscular body, the rounded belly and the massive flank are all still perfectly in their right place.

It takes a great deal of practice to be able to draw moving animals like this, but with practice you'll see yourself improving. Just remember the basic rules of blocking in the shapes of the animal's body. You will need to use photos or pictures from magazines or books. Notice how the back leg on the far side is much further forward than you might imagine – this is because the horse appears to be turning slightly.

Once you've managed to construct a credible attempt at this sort of drawing you'll rightly feel very satisfied.

Drawing plants

Drawing a plant is different from working on other still life drawings because a plant normally has moving parts. A good plant drawing will suggest life and the possibility of change and movement.

Once you have found the basic structure of the plant, you can begin drawing in the features that make the plant unique. Any plant will have at least one dominant feature, whether it is the peculiar shape of the leaves or the unique petals. These features create lines, some of which form very complex patterns.

After the main features have been drawn in, you can turn your attention to how the light falling on the plant creates different patterns of light and shade. This is when your drawing will really begin to come to life.

1

When we look at this Swiss cheese plant, the first things we notice are its leaves. These form ellipses of various sizes and shapes because we are seeing the leaves from different angles. The basic lines of the stem plus the shapes that make up the pot at the bottom form our basic sketch.

2

Now that we have these basic shapes we can begin to draw in the lines of the leaves. If we work carefully here, we can get an accurate impression of how each leaf looks from the angle from which we are viewing the plant. Accurate lines will help make the final drawing realistic and life-like.

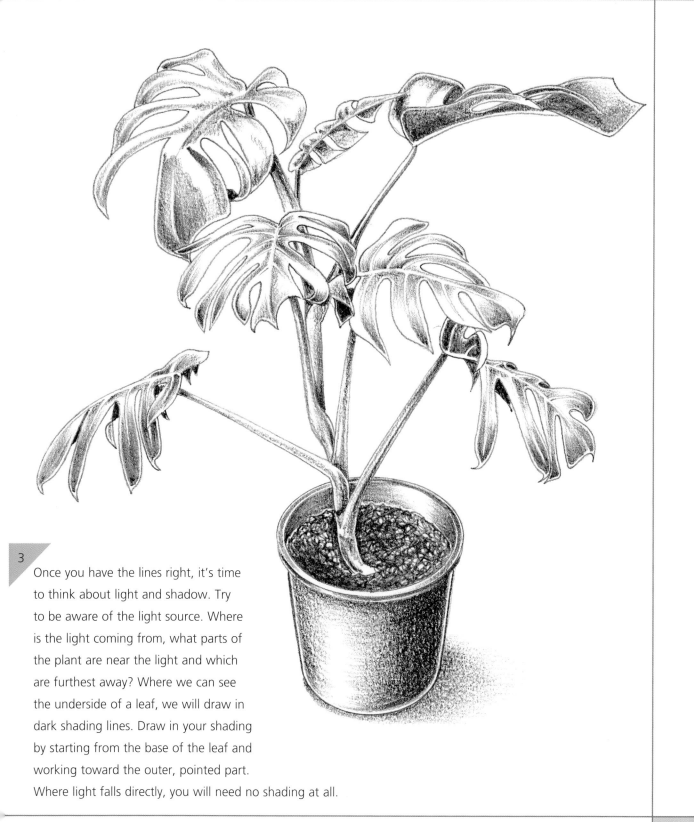

3

Once you have the lines right, it's time to think about light and shadow. Try to be aware of the light source. Where is the light coming from, what parts of the plant are near the light and which are furthest away? Where we can see the underside of a leaf, we will draw in dark shading lines. Draw in your shading by starting from the base of the leaf and working toward the outer, pointed part. Where light falls directly, you will need no shading at all.

Daffodils are such an amazing shape, with their slightly pointed leaves and trumpet-shaped flowers. Make sure that you use initial guidelines to help you hold the whole shape of the flower together and to keep the various elements in proportion to each other.

1

Let's look at the basic shape of this daffodil as seen from a three-quarter angle and slightly from above. The centre, or trumpet, of the flower appears as a slightly ovoid shape, with the characteristic outer petals forming almost the shape of a star. Drawing guidelines from the centre of the study to the outer points of the petals will help us focus on the location of the petals as well as helping create a sense of balance for the final drawing.

2

Now the characteristic features of the daffodil really begin to take shape. The long, spiked leaves are traced in and the petals become well delineated. We add the basic shapes of the stamen and begin to get a sense of the jagged outer edge of the trumpet.

3

Having made a good outline of the flower and its leaves, we can start to think about shading. Once again, think about where the light is coming from. Where does it fall most directly on the plant, and where is there relative dark? Notice that the leaf on the right is beneath the flower head, so it receives little light. The tops of the centre petals, on the other hand, are quite light, and less shading will be needed for these. The trumpet, because of the angle from which we are viewing it, requires a great deal of shading, especially in the inner part, from which the stamen emerges. Note that, even in the finished drawing, the lines need to be well delineated.

Roses are complex flowers to draw, although they have been beautifully depicted by artists such as Renoir and Redouté. At first glance, the basically round shape and intricate folds of the bud seem reasonable simply to draw, but look more closely and you will see that you must capture light bouncing off the smooth petal surfaces.

1

When we look at this beautiful rose, we can see that the initial drawing will be the simplest of the plant studies we have done so far. To begin your drawing, you can start with a simple circle. The unique feature of the rose, its numerous petals, will create amazing patterns of light and shade, but for now you need only draw in the most basic outline of the shape of the petals. The single guideline shows the line of the stem, which forms a kind of centre of gravity for the rose.

2

As we begin to look at the individual petals of the rose, we see what a large number of lines they form. First get the basic outline of each petal, and then sketch in the details. All kinds of edges – smooth, jagged, gracefully curving in all directions – begin to appear as you work.

3

Now you are ready to begin the final drawing. Because this is a dark-coloured rose, your study will require lots of relatively dark shading, with fewer light areas than the daffodil we worked with earlier. As always, however, we must pay attention to the source of light – which parts of the rose are furthest from the light, which part is hidden by other parts, and which part receives the most direct light? Notice that the upper stem, just beneath the flower head, is entirely dark. A thin, light line just inside the outline gives a sense of roundness to the stem. The best way to begin shading the petals is to start from the base and work your way upward, outward, or down, depending on the direction the petal is facing. Make sure the basic lines are dark and well-defined so that they are not overwhelmed by the shading – the shape is extremely important to the final impression.

Detailed features

Remember that a plant is a living object with moving parts; proper attention to shading will add to the impression that you have captured the subject at a unique moment in time. And take into account that the Swiss cheese plant isn't just a plant with leaves, with gaps. The gaps are also part of the drawing and so while you are drawing the leaf you're also drawing the gaps. Make sure you're happy with their shape too.

As we've already noted, the trumpet of the daffodil requires a great deal of shading. It's easy to see, in this enlarged version, just how much care has been taken with this shading, and how the highlight brings the flower to life. There is no particular pattern to the jagged edge of the trumpet, it really is quite random.

Unlike the daffodil, the petals of the rose are wrapped around one another, rather like the leaves of a cabbage. The petals towards the centre of the rose become smaller and more tightly packed. This gives the impression of the rose's centre being very complex, but in reality it is still one petal inside another. Understanding what you are seeing and not being intimidated, is the key to drawing the small details at the very centre of the rose.

This enlargement shows the central part of the flower head, and we can see here how the petals overlap one another. Although the flower as a whole seems to be quite delicate, the petals themselves are actually quite strong and each one stands apart from its neighbour. The outside petals of a rose head open up and lie fairly flat, but those inside are smaller and stand up more as they get toward the centre of the rose.

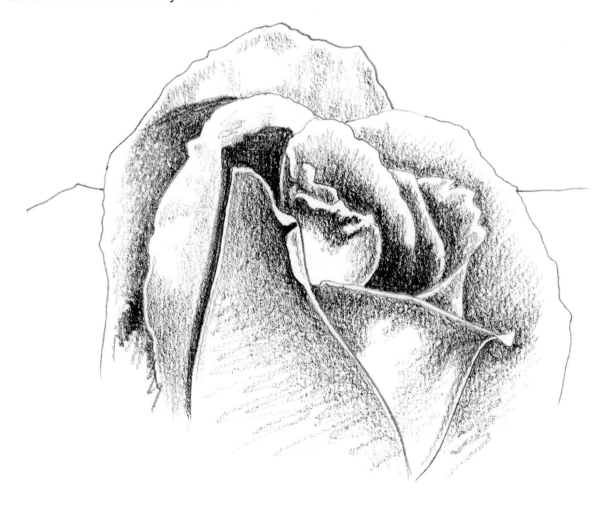

Gallery

This potted cactus gives an opportunity to think about basic shapes, lines, shading and detail work. Because we are looking at it slightly from above, the plant looks somewhat shorter than it would if we were seeing it from a side view. One way to begin capturing the plant's form might be to draw in the lines of the pot, followed by the general shape of the plant itself. Next look closely at the stems and trace the outlines as they appear from your point of view. Notice the lines that are formed by the intersection of the stems and the soil in the pot. Once you have a good outline of the plant you can begin to think about shading.

The ridged parts of the plant are heavily shaded because of the curved shape and the way the light falls on them. Continuous shading, using the flat side of the pencil, is a good way to create these gradual changes of light and dark. Each ridge has a highlight – the ones closest to the front have more light falling upon them. A scribbling technique is called for in drawing the soil - notice the little circles that look like grains of sand. When you are satisfied with the shading, it is time to look at the detail work of the spines. Those that spread out from the top of the plant can be drawn with single lines. Making them of different lengths and going in all directions gives a sense of life and potential motion to the study. Spines that appear nearest to us, at the front of the plant, need to stand out from the background. The best way to do this is to draw a slightly thicker spine with a clear outline.

We can tell from this drawing that it is a bright sunny day because the light is shining so strongly – notice the shadow against the wall of the house. We get the impression of the individual plants, almost just a suggestion, a feeling that they are randomly drawn, but then look harder and some of the flowers are well-controlled drawings – the flower heads have definite shapes. Other flowers blend in one with another.

The balance of this drawing is good because at the front of the window box some of the stems trail downward and their leaves give a shadow on the box itself. Others plants, however, stand tall and erect and therefore give height to the study.

The tonal values on the plants are very delicate and understated, yet we get an impression of a mass of colour.

Landscape

In our minds landscape suggests trees, fields, lakes and mountains. Actually it is far more than that. Landscape encompasses all of those as well as town, cityscapes and seascapes. That makes it a huge subject. You'll find ample resources for these in your home, from books, magazines and photographs, but you can, of course, go out with your sketch pad and draw what you see around you.

If you are new to drawing outside, or even if you're copying from a book or photograph, don't be too adventurous to begin with. At first, try doing some drawings of trees from your garden if you have one, or some farm buildings or even a country lane. For a complete contrast you could then embark on a drawing of a mountain vista, or perhaps a distant lakeside scene – use a magazine picture for inspiration if need be. At this point you will face new challenges with perspective and we will be looking at that over the next few pages.

Use your viewfinder (see page 30) to gain the best composition, and make lots of simple studies before attempting a serious drawing. The important point is to plan your drawing well and then to enjoy it.

We do need to say a little more about perspective here as many of the drawings you will be looking at will need a basic knowledge of the subject.

● First there is the horizon – where the sky meets the land or the sea.
● Now imagine you are looking at a row of posts disappearing off into the distance, or a row of trees doing the same. Where they meet the horizon is the vanishing point.
● The horizon line is your eye level.

Always remember, distant figures appear smaller and also fainter, but have the same shape and proportions as they would close up.

More about perspective

We've already looked at horizon lines and vanishing points. Now look at this drawing and you can see so clearly what it's all about.

You can see that as anything gets further away, it also gets smaller. Now take a ruler and you can follow the line from the angled edges of all the chimneys. Also from the tops of the windows, from the bottom of the windows, from the bottom of the building and the line of the path, all of these lines will meet. And where they meet is the vanishing point. It's the point on the horizon at which parallel lines converge.

Now draw a horizontal line straight through this vanishing point. This is the horizon line, or eye level. The horizon line

in perspective drawing is a horizontal line across the picture. It is always at eye level – its position establishes where we seem to be looking from, from a high place, such as a bridge, or from close to the ground.

We will look at this description of how to find the vanishing point and the horizon line again. The more you see it and read it, the more familiar it will become and then the easier it will be. Soon you'll find that you are working it all out without needing any instruction.

Remember, you can always simply draw what you see if you find that easier.

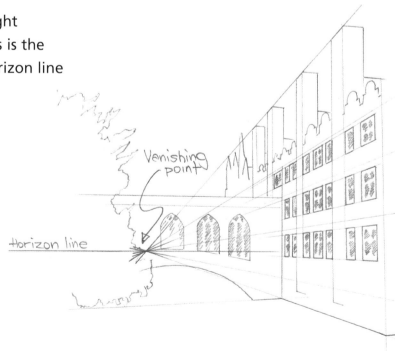

We are looking at this picture from an angle. We have already seen that the buildings on the right of the drawing have very clear perspective lines for you to follow. If you were able to see the buildings beyond the bridge you would simply continue those lines until you reached the vanishing point. The windows and the towers also follow the same lines – you can still see the guidelines lightly drawn in.

The bank nearest to us is also at an angle, albeit a less marked one. Eventually, had we been able to see directly ahead and if the waterway continued straight, the two banks would eventually meet at the vanishing point. However we know that the waterway changes direction after the bridge.

The small walkway over the water, known as the Bridge of Sighs (after the Bridge of Sighs in Venice), is almost a straight ahead view.

Making the initial blocking in drawing for this study, will take some time. It's best not to bother with any detail at all until you have all the main

building work correct. So complete the lines for the bank, the building itself (St John's College, Cambridge), including the upright sections, and the small bridge over the waterway.

Once all this is finished then you can have fun putting in the windows, the bank on the left-hand side, and the trees. Not forgetting, of course, the punter taking his tourists on a sightseeing tour! You may remember we saw this small group and the punt earlier when we were looking at the use of the viewfinder and framing interesting subjects.

Drawing trees

The oak tree is an ideal example when beginning to tackle the subject of trees. You will notice that the overall shape is broadly simple and symmetrical. An important point to remember is that all trees have a characteristic appearance.

Some people are able to recognise trees as they travel around, such as ash trees, elms, beech trees, chestnuts and all manner of other trees. When you've finished your drawing it should be apparent which tree you have drawn.

1

Begin with a long vertical line around which to draw the two balanced outlines and the trunk. The shape is similar to an inverted heart shape or a spade on a playing card. Again we are simplifying our task by using a geometrical image, and at this stage we are avoiding the need to cope with any detail.

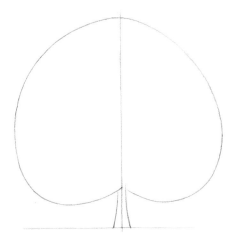

2

We can now vary the outline using the basic shape as a guide. You can develop the overall effect by drawing a very wavy line close to the guideline and also by adding the branches reaching out in all directions. Be careful not to make the branches too symmetrical, and remember that branches and twigs always taper as they grow. The vertical branches must appear related, even if not connected, to the trunk.

3

Now our oak tree is taking on a characteristic appearance. Note where the light falls and ensure that areas of shade are darker in tone as a contrast, for example on the trunk and lower branches.

The dense summer foliage is fairly easy to achieve. Experiment with tiny elliptical movements or scribble effect with the pencil to give the impression of leaves, rather than attempting an accurate record of each leaf as portrayed in a photograph.

It's always good to be able to put your tree into an appropriate scene. The horizontal bench emphasises the vertical lines of the trunk, and makes the oak tree appear even more magnificent.

We begin our drawing of the poplar in the same way as the oak tree, by first observing the characteristic overall shape. Remember that light strikes any object at an angle and your shading must be consistent, for example on the trunk, otherwise your picture will not make sense.

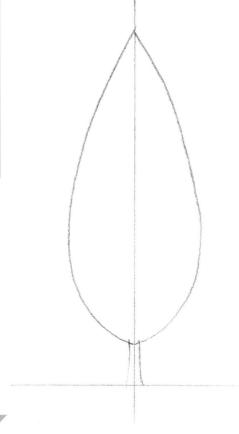

1

A mature poplar forms a shape similar to a feather held upright. Begin the drawing with a vertical line to mark the centre axis, and a horizontal line to indicate the ground out of which the tree grows. Carefully draw in the feather shape, tapering it at the top while making sure the foliage is in correct proportion to the trunk. As we know, care at this stage results in a satisfactory finished picture.

2

In this second stage, and using the basic outline, you can add the wavy outline of the foliage. As with the oak tree the first lines are only a guide that can be crossed both in and out as you draw. This makes our tree instantly more interesting and true to nature. Even a little extra landscape can be sketched in. Make the angle interesting.

3

Now we can complete our poplar tree! As before a realistic representation of the leaves is not required, nor is it desirable. Try experimenting with scribble effect, using varying grades of pencil.

Use an H grade pencil where you want to indicate the delicate foliage at the top of the tree, and you can try using various grades of softer B pencil for the darker and heavier tones towards the base.

Light falls, of course, on the top side of the leaves and so to suggest the upper surfaces these areas need to be left unshaded.

Carefully position more depth of tone in areas where the light is less or does not reach at all.

Finally a few more details angled from the base of the tree set it off well in its landscape.

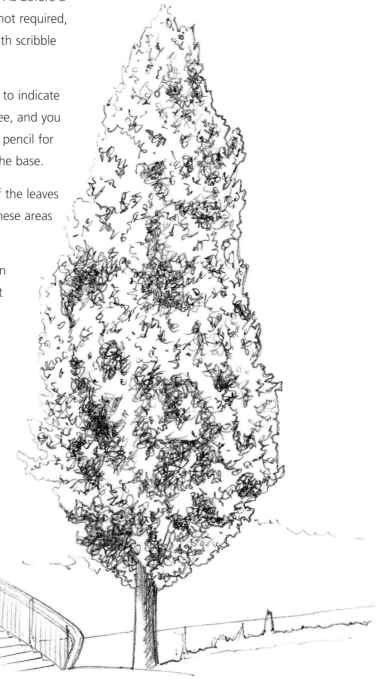

The Scots pine presents a new challenge, but as we know, initial careful observation and identifying the geometric shapes within the object, provides the key to a successful drawing.

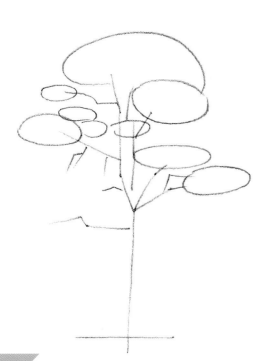

1

We can immediately see that the Scots pine is not a symmetrical shape, but we begin, as is usual; with the horizontal ground line and can place the vertical line at a right angle to it. The tree has a strong skeletal appearance and so try to continue the single lines to show the direction and length of the vigorous horizontal and vertical branches. Then, we indicate the position of the foliage masses and the smaller branches in relation to the main branches with lightly drawn ovals.

This provides the basic outline.

2

At the second stage define the outline in the now familiar way by starting to draw the trunk, following the guideline. Using a fine pencil the outline of the foliage is drawn. Here the initial guidelines can be less closely followed as you sketch in both foliage and the thinner branches. Even the ground at a strong angle to the trunk can be suggested now.

3

At the third stage, after carefully choosing the direction of the light source, using grade B soft leaded pencils to shade will enhance the effect. The well-defined contrast of dark and light in the foliage and on the trunk and branches is extremely important in achieving a representation of this most magnificent of trees.

A bleak and mountainous landscape in which our Scots pine stands alone is suggested with a minimum of simple lines.

Detailed features

In previous detail sections we have shown the more intricate parts of previously presented drawings. It seems more appropriate here to look at sections of trees generally.

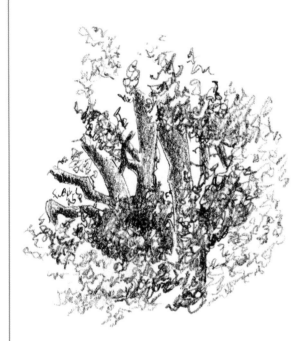

This is a section of the oak tree and from this view we are able to see into the very centre where there is little sun so it is quite darkly drawn. The branches are old and somewhat gnarled and have thick foliage growing around them. To represent the heavy foliage, use a variety of pencils and a scribble effect. Even although it is so shady you can still see some highlights on the branches.

We don't see any branches on this section of tree. What we do see is a very substantial trunk. A branch has probably broken off just below where the leaves start to appear. The light source is coming from the right, causing a strong shadow from hanging leaves.

This is the Scots pine and we can see the section from the lower branches. Interestingly its shape is, a very acceptably balanced tree, although we might wonder about the shadow and where it is coming from.

When we are drawing a tree like this we might not think of including branches that appear dead. But of course trees do have dead branches and we know that on the full-sized tree a few pages earlier, there was a much larger dead branch just below the one we see here and we know that on the full-sized tree a few pages earlier we noticed there was a much larger dead branch just below the one we see here. Dead branches are not disguised by foliage and so you need to take care that the shape is accurate and believable. Remember that the branches taper away toward the tip. The tone on dead branches might be less vigorous than elsewhere and sometimes a tiny bit paler.

Gallery

An old wall leads the eye to a clump of
Scots pines: they are at the foot of a hill
(suggested by cross-hatching which fades
away), and are definitely in the shade as
there is no highlight here at all.

Now that you've spent some time looking at the structure of trees and how best to draw them, maybe it's time to think about drawing some trees in a landscape.

The top drawing of the river running under the bridge is a typical sight on many country walks, and there is an added point of interest - the bridge.

The trees in the drawing are well-balanced on the left hand side, and beyond the bridge, they reach a considerable height. In the foreground, the tree nearest to us is rather low and shrub like. We don't really see a lot of branches in this drawing, suggesting high summer – and this is backed up by the very strong sunlight coming from the right side.

There are no reflections on the water, suggesting that the water is moving fairly rapidly.

In the drawing below, there are reflections on the water of trees on the hills across the lake (these are very rough suggestions of pine forests). Notice how the reflections are wider than the actual groups of trees and fainter and fluffier, suggesting a very light ripple on the water.

The tree in the foreground still has plenty of branches showing. Again the sun is coming from the right side of the drawing.

Cityscapes and seascapes

Now that you're about to look at cityscapes and seascapes, a few more guidelines on perspective will be helpful. We've already mentioned aerial perspective in connection with distant objects appearing less well- defined and how to work out single point perspective (or linear perspective) – remember the exercises in the Still life section (pages 96–97). Multi-point perspective is employed when there are two or more vanishing points. The drawings on the next pages use a variety of different types.

Skyscraper cities are usually built on a grid, and so the diagonal lines which you can see in this blocking in drawing will diverge to the horizon line on the left side of the page. If you follow these lines with your ruler you'll see that the vanishing point is on the waterline. The lines going in the other direction, i.e. to the right hand side of the page, will also meet eventually on the same horizon line, but it will be way off the page.

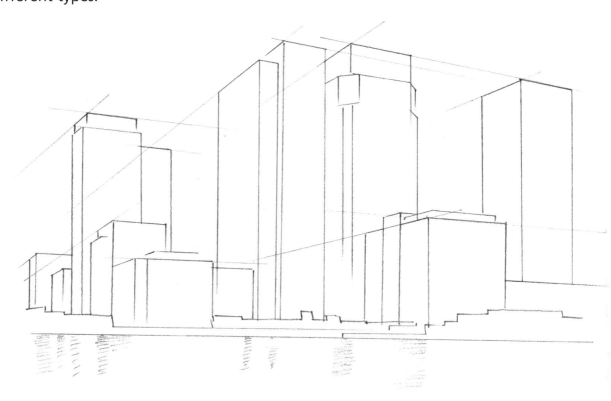

The buildings in this scene are all classic cubes and the perspective here is simple perspective, that is, one vanishing point. Notice the reflections in the water; you can indicate these by short, sideways zigzag lines with a dark pencil. The reflection becomes more like the scene you are reflecting when the water is very still – when the water is perfectly still, then your drawing will be reflected perfectly, in which case turn your drawing upside down when blocking in the outline to check that the image is accurate. Notice also how the windows in the tower blocks are only indicated by lines and dots. Although we don't actually see the windows, we know they are there.

A village hill

The buildings on this hill employ multi-point perspective, because the buildings are not set on a straight road. First, you should establish your horizon line (or eye level), which in this case is about half way up the chimney nearest to us. Because the horizon is above the houses all horizontal lines, i.e. the top and bottom of the roofs, windows and doors, will be slanting upwards towards the vanishing point. The vanishing point of the first two houses is almost above the first chimney of the thatched roof. All other vanishing points are off the page. Remember to find the vanishing point, draw a line that continues along the top of the roof to the horizon line, and draw another line which continues from the bottom of the roof to the same point. All doors and windows should meet at the same point.

1 From this viewpoint it is quite a challenge, as well as being on a steep hill, the street is also on a bend. The most straightforward way of dealing with this problem is to draw what you see. Roughly block in the cottages as you see them, and put in the lines of the road. Once the street straightens out the houses will line up nicely for you but you will need to persevere to find the right angle for the dwellings at the top of the street. Make sure that each house has the correct proportion, that is, that the top of the roof is parallel with the bottom of the roof and also with the bottom of the house. Also the vertical lines should be at right angles to the horizontal lines. Mark in your features at this point – so that you can see that they fit into the available space.

2

Once you are happy with your outlines then it's time to start working on the details. The three cottages at the top of the street are quite challenging because the perspective causes them to be at a severe angle, especially the third house, but they get easier as they straighten out. You have a thatched cottage at the bottom of the hill and the texture on the thatch is much more rugged than the smooth tiles of the other houses. Use a very soft pencil to create an impression of thatch, but remember it must appear lighter in colour, so leave plenty of white space. Notice how the shadow of each house appears on the neighbouring roof.

Gothic building

The Gothic building is also multi-point perspective because there are a number of angles; looking at the block nearest to us, some of the faces of the building angle away from us (the vanishing point is around the middle ground floor window of the middle block) and others angle towards us (the vanishing point is way off to the right). The vanishing point for the middle block would be just off this page to the right. The horizon line goes through the ground floor windows.

1

There are a number of ways that you can simplify your initial drawing.

You will see on the completed drawing two sets of four arches. The stonework above these arches forms a line that is continued right across the entire building.

Above the windows on the angled part of the building is another line of stonework that, although broken, is repeated at the same level. There is also another line of stonework beneath the top windows.

Bear the above points in mind, when you block in the first rough drawing. Make sure that your vertical lines are all at right angles to the ground.

2

Before you do anything else you should mark up all of the window positions. You don't want to start putting in windows and completing all of the detail and then find that you have run out of space.

You may remember that at the end of the introduction we looked at using a magnifying glass. This may be a time to find that tool to help you to see the details of the roof areas and the chimneys, which are quite intricate.

There is also the courtyard behind the arches. You will need to ensure that your angles are correct here. And note that the building beyond the second set of arches is not the same as the two wings which are nearest to us.

This is a magnificent building to draw and if you follow all the steps you shouldn't find it too difficult.

Seaside town

This seascape is multi-point and aerial perspective, but with this type of drawing it is better to draw what you see. Occasionally you can lose the charm of a drawing by trying to be too technical.

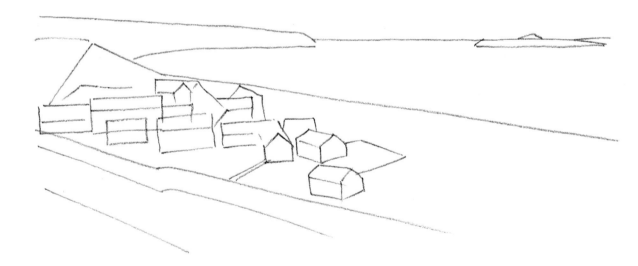

1

Block this scene in simply. Start with important guidelines, such as the horizon, the edge of the sea, and the cliff to the left before you begin to add any of the buildings.

This landscape employs aerial perspective. This means that objects appear less distinct the further away they are from you. So, for example, if there were houses on the island, they would be indistinct in comparison to the houses in the foreground.

2

The sea is quite still – we can see a slight shadow from the island. The edge of the sea shows movement and it is easy to imagine a slight ripple here as minuscule waves lap gently at the water's edge. It is a still calm day, maybe a little overcast. This is shown by the absence of strong shadow on the houses.

The houses in this drawing present multi-point perspective because they present at different angles. However, they are so small that you would probably do well to draw them from observation. They are drawn very simply so as not to be crowded with too much detail.

Detailed features

This is the first of the cottages beyond the bend on Gold Hill in Shaftesbury. The first important point to be aware of, is how steep the hill is on this lane. The road falls away quite dramatically beyond the door.

On the previous page the roof tiles were barely indicated. Here they are slightly clearer, as are the door and the windows.

This is the very first cottage in our original drawing. Now the roof tiles are much clearer – they are individually marked. This cottage doesn't have small leaded window panes as do most of the other cottages. The angle is slightly different here to the original because the front door is masked by foliage.

This is the arched window from the Gothic building – we have a good idea now of the architectural design. This piece has been redrawn for the close-up in order to show that it isn't actually necessary to be so precise in a drawing – it would not have been possible to include all this detail in the previous drawing unless it had been a much larger work.

Again, this detail is from the roof of the Gothic building. You can see clearly now that the stonework around the base is actually a stonework balustrade. The angles are much clearer, as is the decorative brickwork on the chimney.

This detail is from the low block on the centre right of our cityscape. We can now clearly see the two bushy trees at the side of the building. The windows are still not clear and we should probably assume that there are windows all around the building between the horizontal concrete ribs.

Gallery

This is a coppiced willow, or the Purple Osier. Part of the willow family, it is used for coppicing because of its very low branches. This one is alone, in the middle of this landscape scene. Notice how strong the shadow is beneath the tree.

When drawing this tree, you would probably want to begin with a shape that is almost a circle. As with the Scots pine, you would need to block some of the branches in at an early stage.

Probably the most famous clocktower in the world, Big Ben is the name of the bell inside the clock at Westminster Abbey.

If you were looking at one face of this tower straight on you would draw a vertical line from the very top, down through the centre of the clock, and right down to the bottom of the drawing.

You can still do this, but your line won't go through the centre of the clock. Instead it will go much nearer to the edge of the clock, between the hour marks and the minute marks. But it will give you a guideline to work from.

Now that we know all about ellipses, we'll know that because we're looking at the clock face from below, it isn't actually a circle but an ellipse. The clock face on the narrow side is more easily recognised as an ellipse.

Perspective comes into play here, as we would expect. The vanishing point will be some distance away up in the skies above Westminster.

When you begin drawing this building, block in simply with the tower (which is a cube), the clock faces on their cube, and then the turret. Once you have your shape correctly portrayed, then you can add the detail.

Figure drawing and portraiture

Many people find that drawing the human figure is the hardest subject of all, yet it can also be very satisfying once the difficulties have been overcome. Life classes are, of course, ideal to help you on your way, but we don't always have the time for this and indeed some people prefer to learn at home.

You could try asking friends or family to allow you to draw them, and anyway start observing people. Take a sketch book out with you and make studies of people you see in cafes or in the park. And you can make use of the time you spend travelling, such as on trains or in airports (what better way of passing away the hours if you suffer a delay at the beginning of a holiday).

Another good idea is to look at art books. See how the great artists have drawn the human form. You can also make studies of your own in the style of famous artists. There's nothing wrong with copying; in fact it's a very good way of learning and the more you do copy the well known artists the better you will become. Consider Hans Holbein, who always made highly detailed pencil drawings of his portrait subjects. Although the drawings were studies for his paintings, they stand on their own as independent works of art. Leonardo da Vinci's *Vitruvian Man* is famous for setting down the proportions of the human body which are used by portrait artists worldwide.

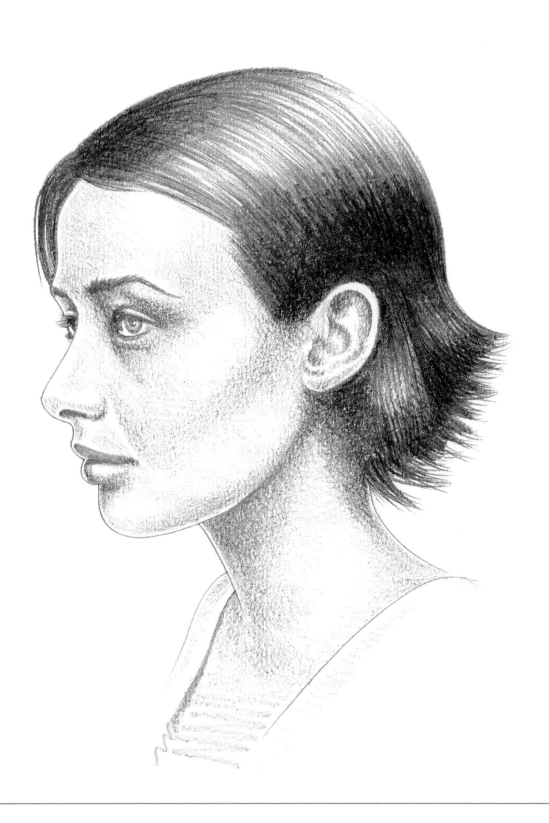

Starting to draw figures

To draw portraits successfully, you need to know a little about proportions of the human body. How do we know how big the head is in proportion to the body?

Generally our bodies follow a pattern. For example, the younger the person the larger the head is in proportion to the body. A baby's head is 25% of the total body size, so it would fit just 4 times into the body. A toddler's head is 20% of the entire body, or fits 5 times into the body.

And a 10-year-old child has a head that is 18% of the body so the head would fit into the body 5.5 times.

An adult's head is approximately 13% of the entire body, which means the head fits into the body 7.5 times. A teenager's head is slightly larger in proportion and would fit into the body 7 times.

Notice that the body becomes shapelier as the person grows older.

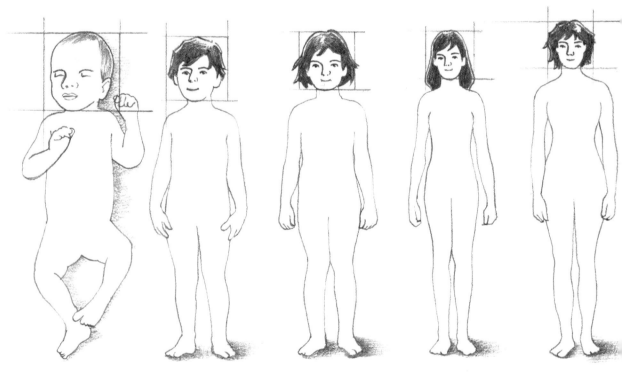

Breakdown of proportions of the body

The average adult human figure is about 7.5 to 8 heads in height. For the beginner that may not sound very helpful, so let's measure those head sizes down the length of the body.

The first head length is obviously the head! The second head length will be close to the central chest line. The next head length will be about waist level, a little above the bellybutton. Note that the elbows are just about level with the waist.

The fourth head length takes us slightly below the groin area; this is roughly where we bend.

You'll notice that we're generalising here – not everyone is perfectly proportioned, and male and female bodies are differently proportioned; for instance males generally have shorter legs than females, whereas women are usually shorter from the shoulders to the groin.

The fifth head length will be a little above the knee and the sixth a little below the knee. Then the seventh takes us to the shins. The final half a head will end at the bottom of the feet.

Another measurement that may be useful, is that the shoulders are roughly twice as wide as the head.

Do remember to block your figures in with a light pencil and check these measurements before adding detail to your drawing.

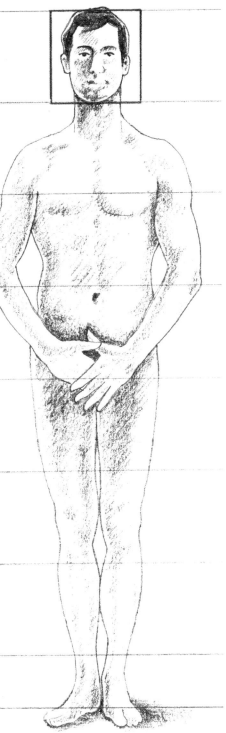

Look carefully at the man and notice how carefully he his balanced on the stool. Your initial observation of his posture and the arrangement of his limbs is very important and will enable you to block in the basic shapes more effectively.

1

You can see from the first blocking process here, that you are marking up just the central body line, the limbs and the head. Note where the joints will be and check that your proportions are right.

2

Now you can see how well the clothed body fits over your initial markings. You need to add the subject's clothing and features at this stage because once you begin adding tone and texture to the final drawing you will find it difficult to add guidelines that were missing.

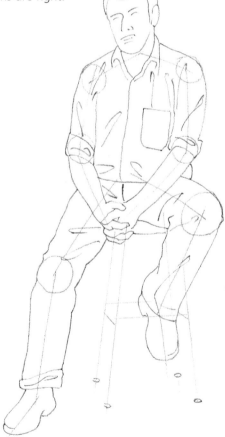

3

This man's posture is very casual but he doesn't seem too happy about having to sit for his portrait – he actually looks quite glum. That's OK for a portrait – we don't need to have smiling faces all the time. Notice how his hands are clasped in front of him.

The light source is easily identifiable here, from the stool legs and by the light shining on the model's jeans and on his shoes.

The central line is interesting because it goes from the model's head and down through his body, and then transfers to the stool.

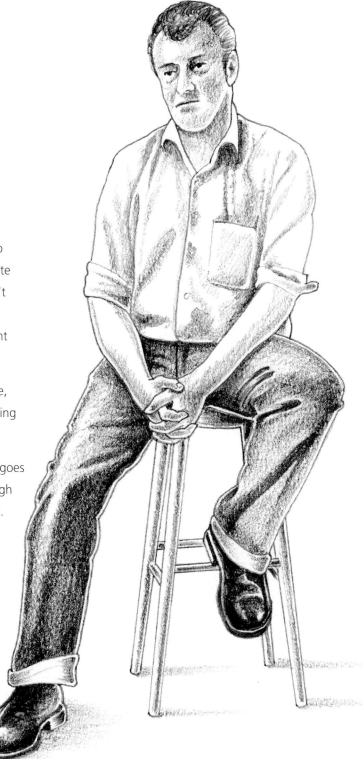

The subject is looking directly at you so this is a good opportunity to draw this happy looking young girl. We will be looking at features later in this section.

Also, you have another opportunity to study an open book. We included an open book at the end of the Still life section. Notice how the pages curve and draw a number of curved lines to suggest multiple pages.

1

Cast your mind back to the Living world section when you were drawing the animals. You used circles in many places around the body to block in the basic shape. It's the same principle here. Think also about geometric shapes – the angles of the legs use two sides of a triangle, and the shoulders, arms and torso make three sides of a box.

2

Keep in mind the rules of blocking in. Just the bare necessities, but make sure the body is in proportion and that you are happy with it before you move on. Remember that the facial features start roughly half-way down the head, and that the eyebrows are more or less level with the top of the ears.

Artist's tip

In this drawing you are studying a variety of elements. For instance look at this girl's legs. Her left leg is in a rather curious position (which looks incredibly uncomfortable). It's good practice, though, to draw subjects in unusual positions as it does make the final presentation more interesting.

3

The hands look very natural; it isn't necessary to put a lot of detail into hands and feet unless you want to bring attention to them. Here the hand conveniently covers the foot so that we don't need to have complicated shapes spoiling the relaxed position.

This is quite a complex drawing to block in. The body is foreshortened so the parts that are nearest to us are much larger than you would imagine. We looked at foreshortening earlier in the book but we know much more about perspective now. It's the same as with a building – objects appear smaller as they move further away.

1

At this stage just mark in the general shapes and joints – circles, triangles and squares. Look long and hard at your model and work out where the limbs are and aim for the angles.

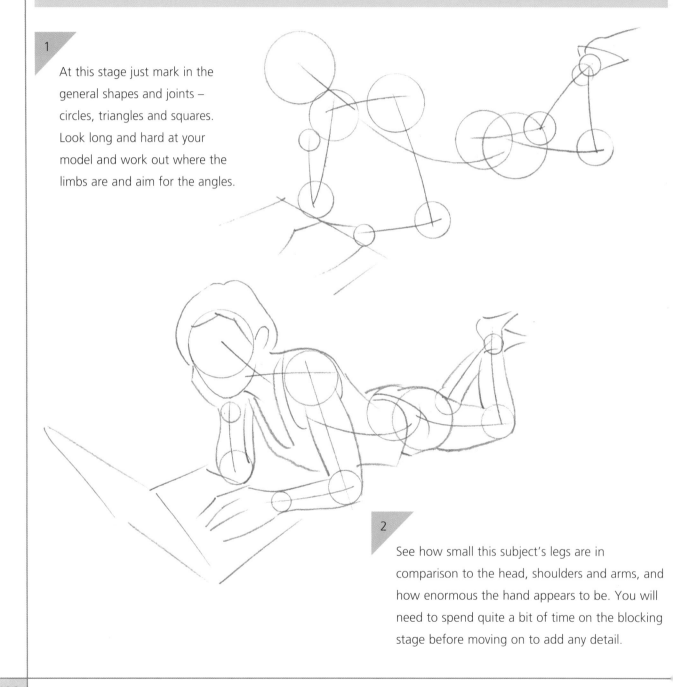

2

See how small this subject's legs are in comparison to the head, shoulders and arms, and how enormous the hand appears to be. You will need to spend quite a bit of time on the blocking stage before moving on to add any detail.

3

We have another opportunity to look at perspective here, this time with a laptop. The rule is just the same as if it were a building, but notice that the lid of the laptop is leaning back slightly – so there are no vertical lines.

The head, in this position, is not quite egg-shaped but more oval, and set at an angle, that makes the ear seem to be sitting on the neck. Notice the angles around the limbs. The upper arm and the forearm make two sides of a triangle, as do the thigh and calf of the left leg. The lower part of the right leg completes the triangle.

When drawing people it's important that the viewer knows why you've chosen that particular person and that particular pose. This young woman seems to be watching something or someone that pleases her and her demeanour and her pose are very relaxed.

1

In this drawing the girl has been very roughly blocked.

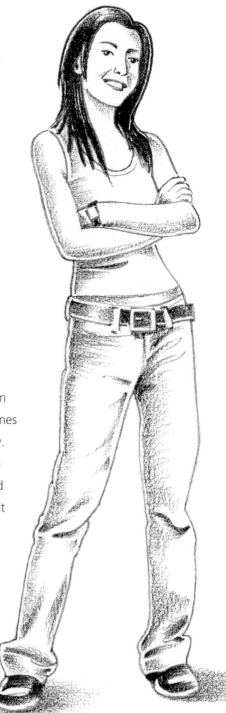

2

Shop windows or photos in fashion and sports magazines are good sources for study. Notice how the jeans lie in folds around the ankle and the knee, and how the belt is just slightly loose rather than fitting neatly around the top of the jeans. The overall impression of this drawing is casual and the clothing should be appropriate.

Remember to check that the child's head is in proportion to his body – it should fit into the body 5.5 times. The proportion of bat to the child is also important; the total length of this bat is around half the boys' height.

1

This boy has been very roughly blocked in. Once you have the angles right then you are ready to start adding detail to your drawing. Don't add any detail until you're happy with the basic shape.

Artist's tip

Notice how the boy is getting ready to move; his feet are not standing square on the ground. Since he isn't wearing shoes it's worth spending time making sure the feet are right. His facial expression shows great excitement – he's going to hit this one really well!

2

It's important to notice the clothing of people and to study the different fabrics and how they lie on the body. The weight and texture of the fabric controls the way it drapes or folds. You control this appearance with the way you add texture. You can suggest whether the material is wet or dry, creased or ironed.

Gallery
Moving figures

One important point to remember when drawing moving figures, is that when we are moving we need to be balanced. If we're not balanced, we'll fall over. This woman is holding rather a contorted pose, but she is still balanced. Although her upper body is leaning in one direction, her hips are pointing in the other direction.

The proportions of the limbs and torso are very important in this type of drawing, so try to spend some time observing the figure in order to get it right.

There is a great deal of strength in this body, particularly in the feet and legs. We know this because she is balancing on her toes while holding this difficult position. But notice the delicacy of the hands and fingers. She is concentrating intensely on her stance and pose.

You would probably need to look at photographs in magazines or on the internet to see just how the legs should be placed when running, and also where the arms would be positioned.

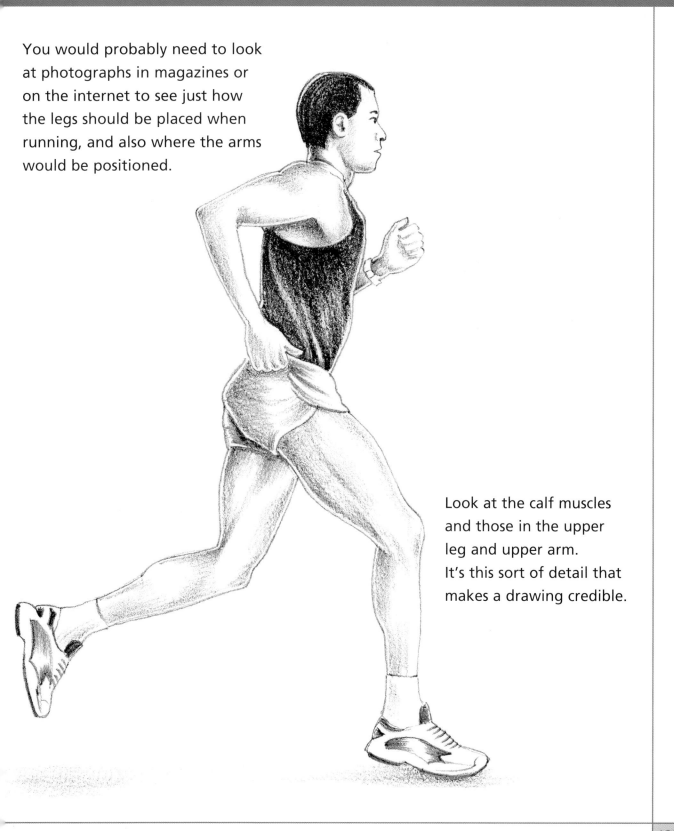

Look at the calf muscles and those in the upper leg and upper arm. It's this sort of detail that makes a drawing credible.

This young woman, possibly playing volleyball, has made a dive in order stop the ball from touching the ground. Notice that her hair is still floating in the air from the speed of her movement.

Her position is obviously unbalanced. We continue talking about the balance point of the body and know that if the body (human or animal) isn't balanced then the body will fall over. This woman cannot maintain this position but then she won't need to. Her eyes are following the ball and her arms are held out to the front to hit the ball, we know that within seconds she will be back on her feet.

This is another drawing of a moving figure where you could look at photographs or pictures of a child actually playing football. Only then will you see where the arms are positioned and how the body transfers the weight from one leg to another. Notice how the eye appears to move from the ball to the area where the ball will be aimed.

The clothes also give a good idea of movement. It can be challenging at times to find the right sway for the fabric.

Artist's tip

Remember:

- when drawing a child's features, don't be tempted to outline every detail

- think of the head as an egg-shaped sphere

- remember the law of balance and stability

- always draw what you see

- even if you can't see the child's body because his clothes are baggy, try to envisage his shape so that the limbs look lifelike.

This rather contorted exercise is interesting for the artist in a variety of ways. See how the upper part of the leg that is on the ground is foreshortened. Notice also how, looking at the subject from the top of the head, there are no features on the face other than the nose.

This is a complicated action drawing and we have a number of examples of foreshortening. The man with his back to us has two foreshortened limbs. His lower left arm is foreshortened because it is pointing away from us, but only slightly and so the foreshortening isn't very noticeable. His upper right leg, however, is very foreshortened because of his position.

Look at the pressure points here, again of the man with his back to us. His knee, lower leg and foot are pressed to the ground, as is his left forearm. If we look at his balance points he is actually fairly well-balanced. Imagine there are guidelines from his left elbow up across his back to his right shoulder, and also from the top of his head and at right angles to the other guideline, down through his lower spine.

We see very little of his opponent, but he appears to be pushing our main subject, who might just end up on his back.

The human figure

Drawing the human form can sometimes seem like a huge challenge. Clothing hides the form and so drawing the nude is a study of the shape of the body. Drawing a nude model in a life drawing class is obviously the ideal, but this may not be possible and you can learn to draw the figure without a model. Friends or family may be happy to model wearing close-fitting sportswear so that foreshortening and proportion can still be explored drawing arms and legs.

Before you start drawing the nude form you really need to know how the body works. Stand in front of a full-length mirror and lift your arm – notice where the arm swings out, and how it looks when it moves.

Do the same with the leg and notice the hip line. This line is extremely important to an artist, as it is where the body divides in half. The distance from the top of the head to the hip is equal to the distance from the hip to the feet. This woman is all verticals and horizontals and a variety of geometric shapes. She has a wonderful central line going from the top of her head and down the leg to the foot. Her right leg and her arms cross at right angles to the vertical lines of her lower left leg and her upper arms.

There are lots of triangular shapes here; the knee and leg between her chin and her arms, her left shoulder and upper arm, and even her face has a triangular shape below her hairline. The left hip is a circular shape, as are the two shoulder joints and the right knee.

When blocking in a drawing like this, one thing to take care over is that the left leg does pick up again in the right place below and above the arms. To be sure you have this right, draw a continuous line through the arms very lightly so that you can erase the marks afterwards.

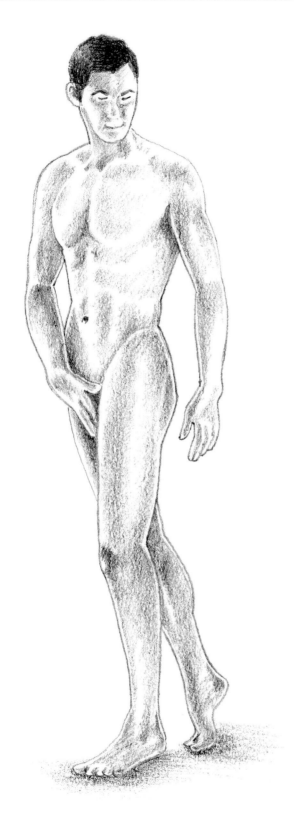

The male torso is less rounded than the female figure – it is angular and strong. Remember there is very little movement in the torso. It can bend to the front and to the back, and to a lesser degree from side to side. It can also twist from side to side, but all of this movement is only at the waist. The upper body and the pelvis do not have movement.

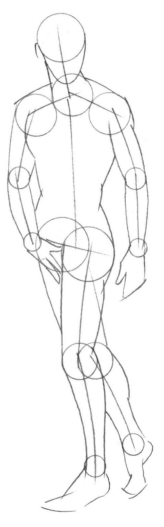

You can see in this drawing that the subject is moving his legs, looking to one side and there is slight shoulder movement, but the torso remains still. The balance goes from the head and down through the left leg.

We've already talked about drawing what you see. In this drawing you see very little of the model. We know she has two legs but we see only one (apart from the toe of her left leg).

This is a drawing about a back. Smooth, shapely and rounded. We see the hint of a breast, but even if we didn't, this is obviously a woman's back. Notice how the line flows from her right elbow down through the arm and the body, and then right along the right leg and back again to continue up the left side of the model. There are no clothes to get in the way of the human form here and this is why so many artists find painting the nude the definitive form of their art.

Gallery

This rather compactly folded-up figure provides the artist with a variety of interesting shapes. Both hands are holding her feet, and the criss-cross of limbs shows interesting geometric shapes. As with the first nude drawing, there are a variety of triangles – the knee, the foot and heel and the torso.

It is important that you draw what you see. Very little of this woman's right arm and shoulder are showing and it's important that when we do see the wrist and hand they are in a credible position. And again make sure that the tiny portion of right knee matches up with the rest of that leg, and indeed that the left leg is accurate.

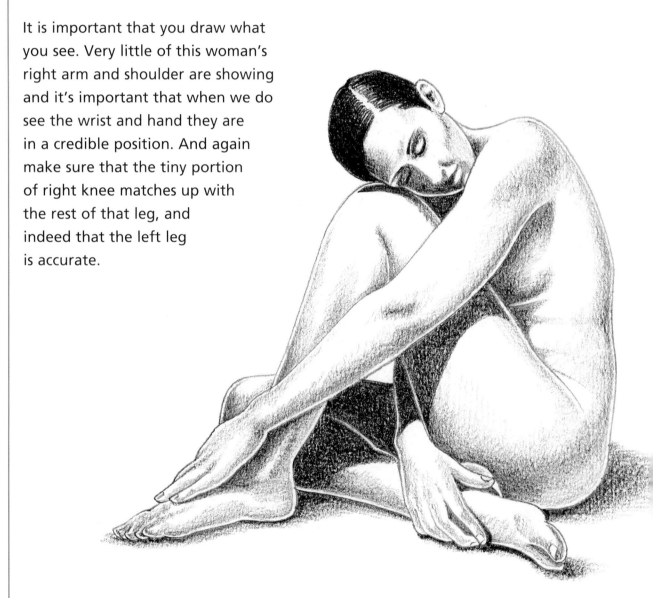

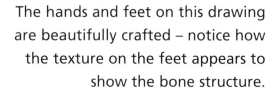

The hands and feet on this drawing are beautifully crafted – notice how the texture on the feet appears to show the bone structure.

When you're blocking this drawing you might think of the general shape as being box-like. Then within that box and continuing beneath it are the strong verticals which are the legs. The arms are also vertical as well as diagonal and the small circular head at the top. There are no facial features to be concerned about.

This model's position is rather like the woman at the beginning of the nude section just a few pages back, but this is a very different representation. The previous drawing had very delicate tone, whereas the tone here is high contrast.

The light source is coming from the observer's right, and is probably a very stark light. This is highlighting in particular the muscles on his left arm, and of course his right side is extremely dark.

Another drawing of a woman with her back to us, but this time she is facing directly away from us. Notice how this drawing is almost symmetrical.

When you are blocking this in you should be aware of the general shapes. The head is almost circular, the shoulders rounded, the arms set at an angle but not quite a triangular shape inside the arms because the body is very curved. The hips form another circle.

The back has to be shaded in a subtle way. This is a large expanse of flesh and if we didn't take care with the texture and shading it could be rather uninteresting. So the left side of the body is quite heavily shadowed because the light source is to the right. Then the crevices are textured with a dark pencil and any bones which might protrude, such as the shoulder blades and the spine, are lifted with much lighter shading.

The hair is a sharp contrast to the body, being fluffy whereas the body is smooth.

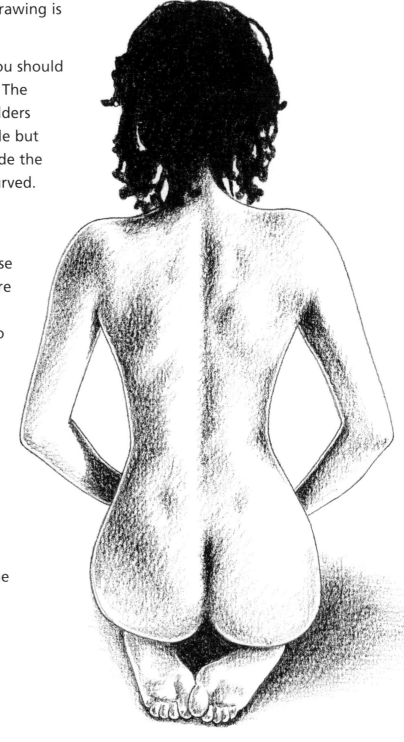

This drawing is based on Rodin's *The Thinker*. Note how the central line goes from his head, which is resting on his right hand, through his left hand, which is resting on his knee, and down to his foot, which is resting on the floor. This relationship between the different parts of the vertical line must be relevant.

Perhaps also relevant is that he has no hair. This gives such a magnificent flowing line from his brow right through to just above his left knee, broken only by the suggestion of the seat he is resting on.

When you block this in, the upper part of the body (from the knees up to the head) is almost square. His limbs are very muscular but he is still quite slender – we can easily see the ankle bone.

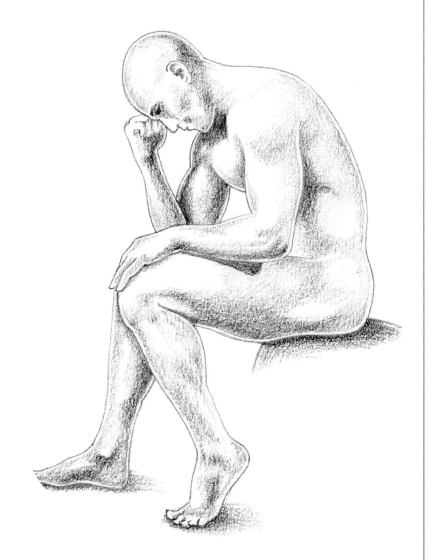

Studies of hands

Some people find hands quite difficult to draw. Certainly if you're new to drawing you might find in the early stages you need to practise, and then practise more.

Draw the hands from various different angles – only the vague outline to begin with. As with the step-by-step we've looked at on previous pages, find your centre line. Add circles for the joints so that you know where all the shapes are going to go before you begin to add any tonal values.

1

Look at the drawing opposite and try drawing this yourself. Begin by looking at the main shapes. Find your centre line – use a box shape for the palm of the hand, and add circles for the joints. Remember that the thumb only has two joints while your fingers have three (counting the connection to the palm).

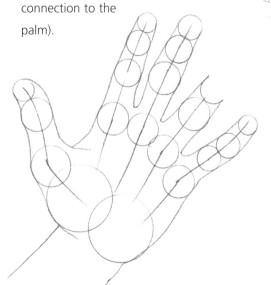

2

When you think you've drawn the basic shape as accurately as you can, fill out the shape a bit more by adding lines and checking angles. Keep looking at your own hand while you're doing this so that you can see where the lines need to go, especially for the joints and the place where the fingers join the palms.

Finish off by adding the detail and the shading.

Now look at these hands.

Look at your own hand and you'll notice wrinkles, shadows, nails, and other details that you can fill in. Make a fist yourself and notice the wrinkles – they change as your tighten and relax your fist. Notice how the wrinkles seem taut at the base of the thumb.

Remember to use a slightly harder pencil to accentuate the wrinkle lines – this helps to show that the lines are tense.

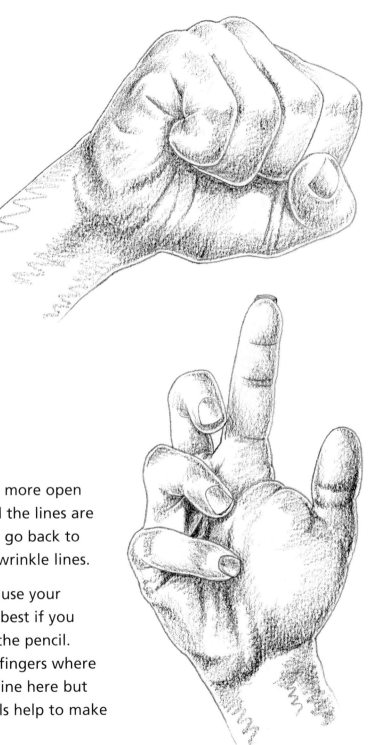

The next drawing shows a slightly more open hand. It is much more relaxed and the lines are less tense. Therefore you can now go back to using a softer pencil to show the wrinkle lines.

Again, you might find it easier to use your own hand as a model – it may be best if you draw the hand that doesn't hold the pencil. Look carefully at the lines on the fingers where the knuckle bends – not just one line here but usually two lines. These tiny details help to make the drawing more professional.

Look at the curve on this thumb. See how the curve extends all the way from the wrist. Examine your own hand held in the same way. Not everyone will have the same amount of curve. Drawing helps you to notice these differences and it is these details that will make your studies more interesting.

Remember to look for the highlights. Here the knuckles are beautifully highlighted – remember there are different ways you can do this:

- You can leave the paper white and build up your tone from the highlighted area
- You can lift the pencil marks off the paper with your putty rubber. You may find you have to redo some of the shading until you become experienced at using this method.

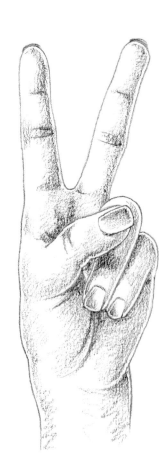

Hold your own hand in this position and look at the shape between your forefinger and middle finger. Some of us have long, thin fingers, while others have shorter, stubby fingers. The type of work we've done throughout our lives also has an effect on the look of our hands. Remember to convey the right impression to the hand you're drawing.

This same information can be shown with the fingernails as well – male, female, child, older person, or even false fingernails. Notice how the hint of a fingernail is shown peeping out behind the tips of the two extended fingers.

In this drawing the wrist looks delicate and slender – spend some time getting the angles right and make sure that the dimensions are correct as well. Hold your own hand in a similar position and check how far down the forefinger the thumb extends. Remember to highlight, particularly on the nails.

This hand is quite chunky. Compare it with your own; the dimensions still need to be correct. It's always good to draw hands holding something; it takes the pressure off getting the fingers to look natural. It also makes the drawing more interesting, and encourages you to study exactly how you do hold an item.

Studies of feet

As with the hands, you'll probably need to spend quite a bit of time practising how to draw feet. Draw them from all angles – each different view produces a very different drawing.

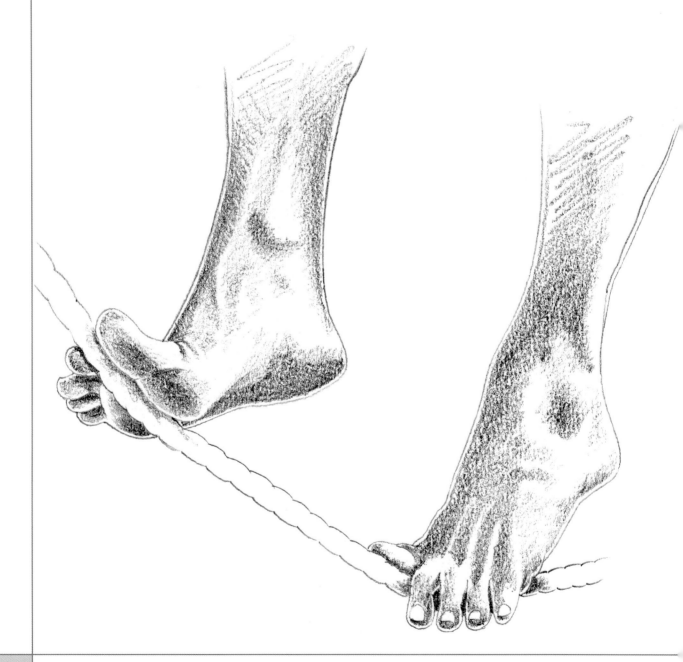

The drawing opposite forces you to study the different angles of the feet. One foot is almost pointed but then the toe is bent upwards over the rope. The other foot shows a very pronounced big toe as well as part of the sole of the foot. So in the one drawing you will need to draw the toes from above and below – and you'll see how different they are.

You can also see that the inside ankle bone is large compared to that on the outside.

Remember that when you are standing, the outside of your foot is usually flat on the ground. The arch of the foot is on the inside, normally raised from the ground. Notice that the big toe is often separated from the other four toes, rather like the thumb is separated from the fingers.

1

Remember to use the same rules and guidelines for starting out on your drawing – draw the main shape, and then add horizontal and vertical lines for guidance. Now start to define the shape by adding texture and tone.

2

When you are drawing feet, try blocking in the toes as small cylindrical forms. Draw the toenails properly as this will help put the foot in perspective. This is important, since all views from the front present the foot in perspective.

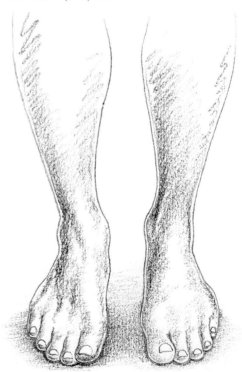

There are no hard and fast rules about the length of toes – sometimes our toes are more or less all the same length – more often the toes are gently shaped, each one a bit shorter than the previous one. Sometimes they lie flat, and sometimes they curl. You can have great fun creating many different studies like these.

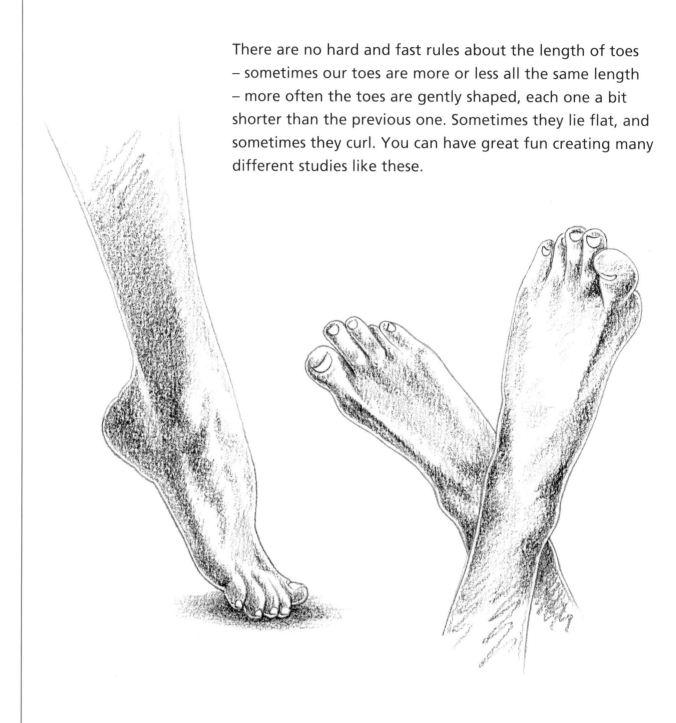

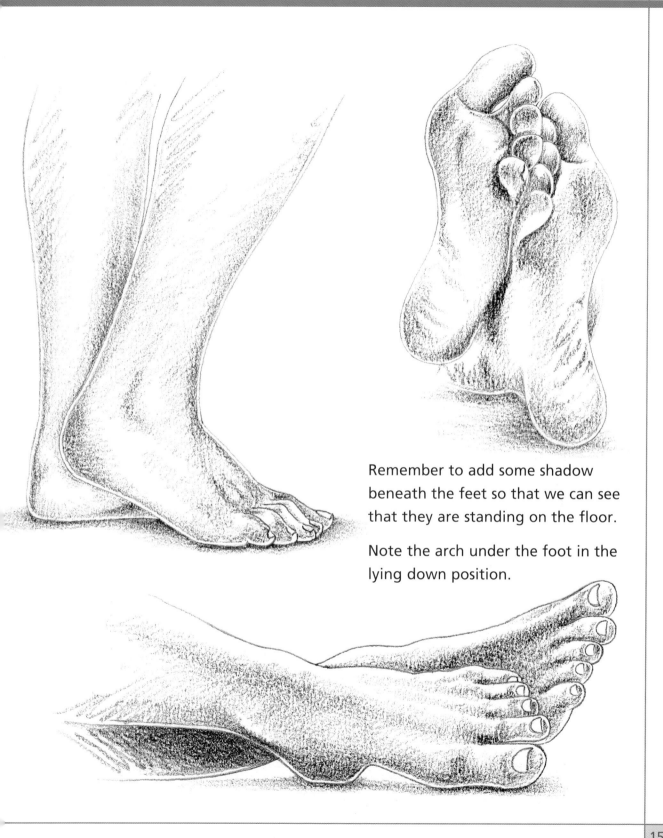

Remember to add some shadow beneath the feet so that we can see that they are standing on the floor.

Note the arch under the foot in the lying down position.

The head

The head is almost a sphere, or egg shaped. It is a bit wider at the top and narrowed at the bottom; but it's a good starting shape for drawing heads.

Generally speaking, the eyes should be placed halfway down the head. An artist will draw a horizontal line halfway down the head, to locate the eyes, and a vertical line down the centre of the head to locate the centre of the features.

In the picture opposite the woman has her head slightly raised, so the eyes will be slightly above the centre and the lower part of the face seems larger and closer to us due to foreshortening.

1

Draw the face with very light strokes, adding the hair and features but no tone at this stage. Make sure that the hair is part of the initial egg shape and not above it – that will destroy the proportions. You can, of course, add volume to the hair.

2

When everything is in the right place you can begin to add shading. Add light tone over the face and in the hair and then begin to add the darker tone. If necessary, use the putty rubber to lighten any area that looks too dark at this stage. Begin to add texture and tone to the main features. At this stage you can strengthen the contour lines and also mark in the eyebrows and nostrils.

3

The finished drawing has the features and shading strengthened.
Remember, you can still remove any excess shading with the putty
rubber to add facial highlights, for instance to the forehead.

This semi-profile view can often make a more interesting drawing than a face viewed from the front. But of course the central vertical line will be no help for aligning the features. Use your pencil to check the distances between the features.

See how in the final drawing the tone has actually been made lighter around the eyes, particularly the eyebrows.

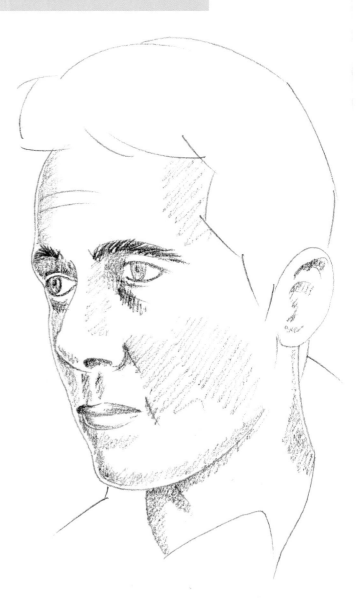

1

Use the blocking-in to position the features and to make sure that the head is angled correctly. Take care that the eyes are not too close together in this semi-profile view.

Artist's tip

Remember that hair grows upwards away from the skull; this man has strong dark hair and the strands are accentuated. Make sure the strokes come out of the head and curve. Leave gaps to obtain the highlights.

2

The temptation can be to shade the face too heavily in the case of a male model. Begin by shading quite sparsely around the areas where facial hair growth is either natural or desired. Finish the eyes by adding highlights and thus giving life and character to the face. Then add further texture or shading only if you feel the drawing requires more.

This drawing shows a woman smiling. It can be a challenge to capture a smile on paper, and of course you do need to ensure that the eyes are smiling as well. If you don't manage that, the drawing doesn't really work.

Smiling, or laughing, is more than just the shape of the mouth. Look at the lines on this woman's face. Look at yourself in the mirror, or photos of people in magazines.

Do the teeth show? Yes, in this drawing they do, but some people manage beautiful smiles even with their teeth tucked well away from sight.

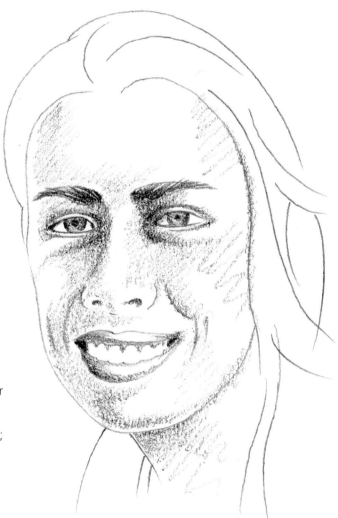

1

When you are blocking in a head, look at the person to see what their most noticeable characteristics are. This woman has very large features; finding their position on the face should be your first step.

2

Now you have to add texture and tone to bring this face to life. If you want to make a point of her beautiful white teeth, you'll need to gently add tone to the whole face, with the exception of any highlighted areas. This model has pretty dimples; use a soft black pencil, probably a 3B or 4B, to give depth to this feature.

Don't forget that the chin needs a highlight, to emphasise the fact that our chins protrude a little.

A middle-aged person is interesting to draw because the face is likely to be beginning to show more lines. Therefore you can introduce more highlights, such as on the chin and above the eyebrows. The receding hairline also gives scope for highlights.

1

A characteristic of this face is that his eyes droop downwards at the outer edge, and the eyelids are quite heavy, in particular his left eye. Block the features in carefully, before adding any age lines, such as those leading down from the nose.

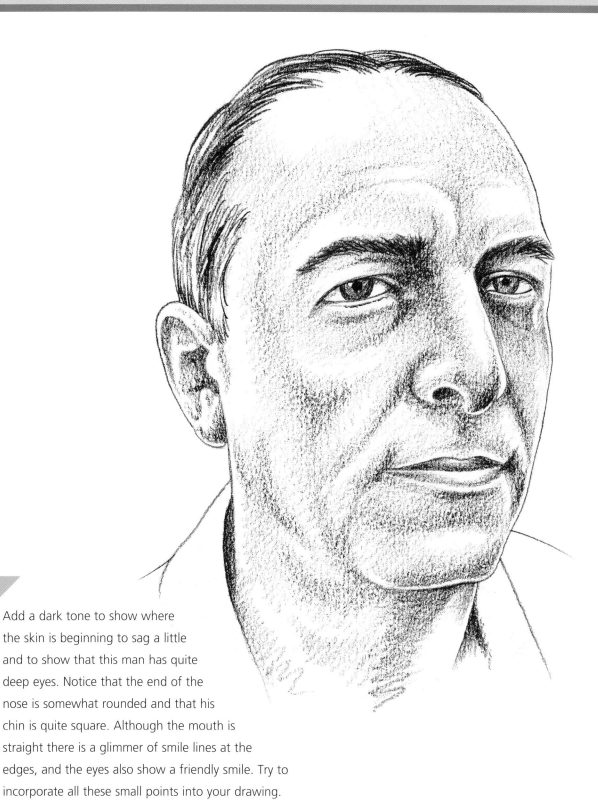

2

Add a dark tone to show where
the skin is beginning to sag a little
and to show that this man has quite
deep eyes. Notice that the end of the
nose is somewhat rounded and that his
chin is quite square. Although the mouth is
straight there is a glimmer of smile lines at the
edges, and the eyes also show a friendly smile. Try to
incorporate all these small points into your drawing.

A general rule is that the corners of the mouth often fall in a line directly beneath the pupils of the eyes. A smiling mouth will obviously stretch a little further. The more you practise drawing people, the easier it will become to notice these points and therefore make your drawings more accurate.

Notice the highlighting on this woman's hair and in her eyes. Details like this bring a drawing to life.

1

This model has her head raised slightly and the important points to remember are that the nostrils will be more visible than usual and all features will be placed higher on the head than normal. Once you've sorted out the correct position for these features you can move on to adding more detail.

2

Drawings of women with long hair usually avoid the need to worry about ears, and this model is no exception (just a tiny bit of ear peeping through). Notice how the wide smile has also caused the nose to be wider than it probably is when the face is resting. Smiling also causes the cheeks to lift and this is shown by the highlights on her cheeks and around the nostrils.

Detailed features

The nose can seem difficult to the beginner, probably because it protrudes. First you need to find the position of the nose on the face. For blocking in, remember that the nose is centred between the eyes and that its narrowest point is where glasses rest. The nose is a vertical form, straight from top to bottom unless the nose has been injured or broken, in which case it might lean slightly to the right or left. At the bottom of the nose are the nostrils – these should be very dark. Very often these are not clearly seen from the front view, depending on the position of the head. Remember that the nose will change shape when the subject is smiling – it will appear wider as the nostrils dilate.

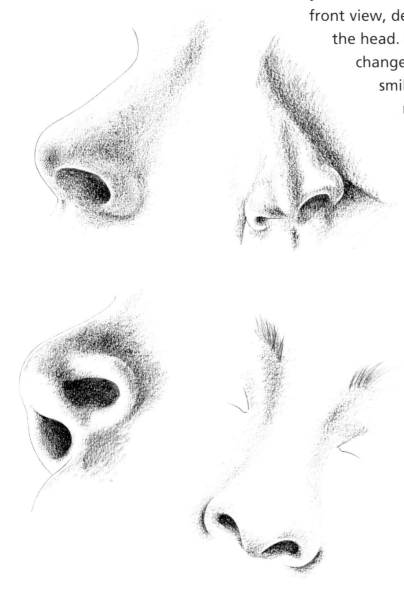

In profile view, the nose is triangular and starts at the bridge between the eyes. It's usually curved, rounds off at the tip and rejoins the rest of the face just above the septum.

Pick out the highlights on the bridge area and have the main highlight on the tip. Check where the light source is coming from – you may need to have shadow on the upper lip. You will need to take care with shading to avoid a flat appearance.

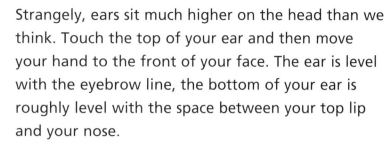

Strangely, ears sit much higher on the head than we think. Touch the top of your ear and then move your hand to the front of your face. The ear is level with the eyebrow line, the bottom of your ear is roughly level with the space between your top lip and your nose.

There are an enormous variety of ear shapes. Some are small and neat, others are large and weather-beaten. Some people have ears that stand well away from the side of the head, or have hairy ears. It isn't easy to see your own ears so you'll have to look in magazines or at photographs. You could ask a member of your family if you might draw their ears.

The rough shape of an ear is an oval disk, or ellipse, the top slanting toward the back of the head. Around the top and back of the ear is an inner line that continues down to the lobe.

In the centre is a circular bowl which is quite deep; you can suggest the shape of this area with texture and shading.

Of course we don't always see the ears in drawings. We may cover them with hair. If the drawing is a profile then we see just one ear. Only when the face is facing fully to the front do we see both ears equally.

In practical terms, eyes incorporate several different shapes and textures to draw. They are also the most expressive part of a person's face.

Look at your own eyes in a magnifying mirror and draw what you see.

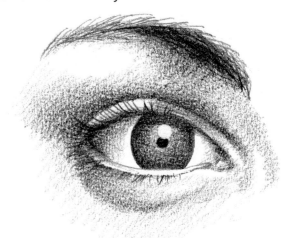

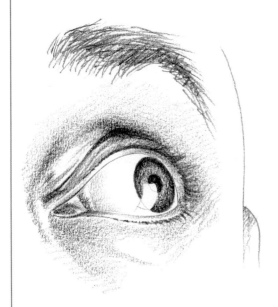

As with any other drawing just sketch in the basic shapes first. Start with a sphere. Draw the eyelids curving over the sphere and then the lower lid, followed by the eyeball, and the round, coloured iris. Remember to add the tear duct where the upper and lower eyelids meet next to the nose. Next draw a line where the eyebrows will be.

Then you're ready to start to add detail. Add the black pupil in the centre of the iris. Notice where the highlight should be in the eye – either leave the paper white or remove any pencil marks with the putty rubber.

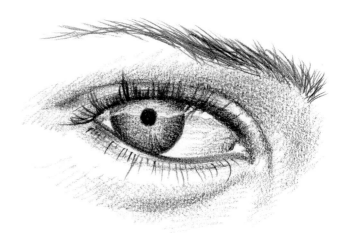

Eyebrows are made up of lots of very short hairs so make sure that your pencil work shows these. Use a 2B or HB pencil and keep it sharp.

Remember that people's eyes are not always a mirror image; sometimes a person has one eye that droops at the outer edge and our eyebrows can be slightly different in shape.

Study your own mouth in a mirror. Mark on your paper with a light line where you want the mouth to be.

Start with the corners of the mouth and draw in the line between the lips. This is the strongest line on the mouth so try to get a good shape here.

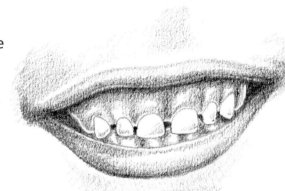

Now form the upper lip, developing the shape as you form the line. Remember to include the septum that runs vertically from the nose to the lip. When you add the lower lip, remember to include some shadow beneath the lip and then you'll need a highlighted area on the chin.

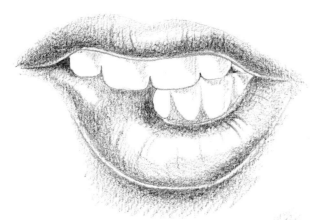

If you draw the mouth in profile you might want to consider if the lips are pouting, or if they naturally protrude.

There is a lot more to drawing mouths than just the lips, however. You need to think about open mouths and teeth. Then there is the matter of bristles above the upper lip of a man (and on the lower part of the face).

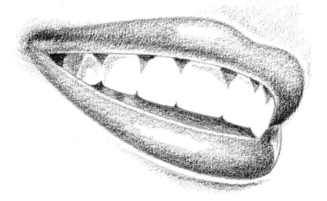

Gallery

Whenever a person sits in a position such as this, for instance with the hands clasped in front of the leg, there is tension in the body. Notice how the shoulders are pulled forward. It would be easier to see this if the woman was not wearing a shirt, but you can still tell there is tension between the hands and the shoulders from the way the back is rounded.

The right foot might appear to be in a strange position but it is correct. Try sitting in this position yourself and notice how the foot twists. As we've noticed before, whenever the limbs bend we are likely to see triangles. In this drawing we also see triangles where the sleeve and the front of the shirt meet the thigh. Finally, we can tell it is a sunny day because the hat is causing a shadow to fall on the subject's hair.

The subject in this drawing is sitting at an unexpected angle. Notice how small his head is in proportion to his feet, and how large his hands are. This is exaggerated perspective.

If we had been looking at the subject in a normal view, that is, from the front and level with him, we would probably be aware of foreshortening in the upper leg limbs. However, because we are so far below him, that effect is barely noticeable.

What we do notice is the ellipse of the stool, and the rather strange formation of the legs of the stool. And because we're looking up at his face, the eyes and eyebrows are high on his face and we clearly see the nostrils.

It's good practice to attempt unusual positions – don't expect wonders straight away, but practice makes perfect!

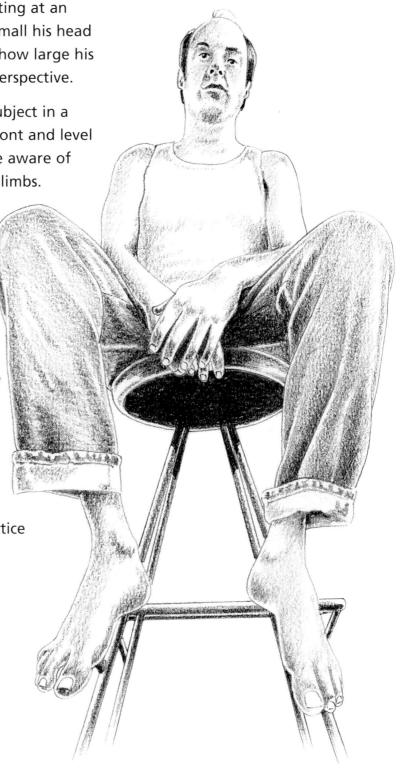

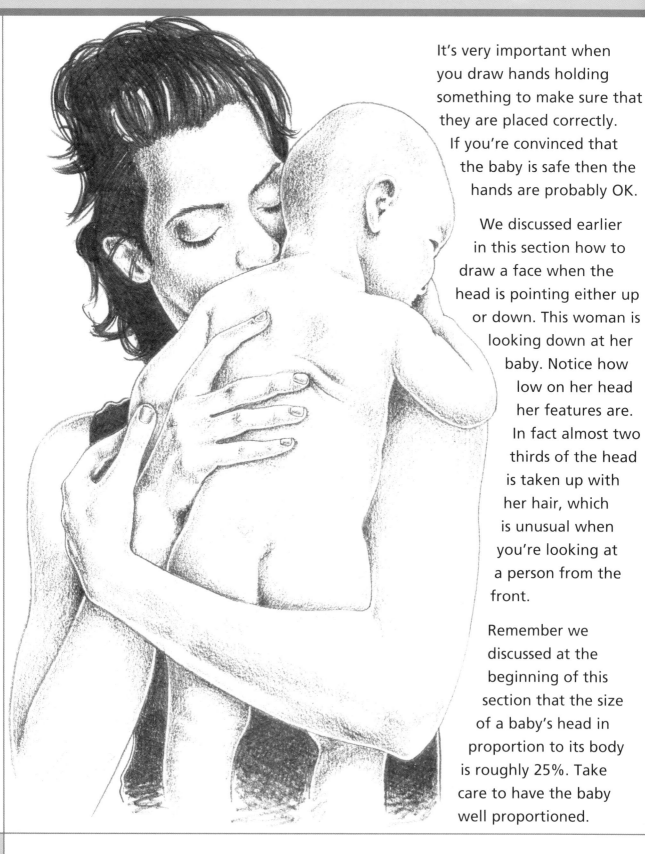

It's very important when you draw hands holding something to make sure that they are placed correctly. If you're convinced that the baby is safe then the hands are probably OK.

We discussed earlier in this section how to draw a face when the head is pointing either up or down. This woman is looking down at her baby. Notice how low on her head her features are. In fact almost two thirds of the head is taken up with her hair, which is unusual when you're looking at a person from the front.

Remember we discussed at the beginning of this section that the size of a baby's head in proportion to its body is roughly 25%. Take care to have the baby well proportioned.

You'll probably need to look at this drawing for quite a while before even figuring out exactly how this chap has positioned himself. It was probably drawn from a photo because no one would be able to hold that position for very long.

He can't be standing because his feet are in the wrong place. He's obviously stretching out his arms and that is mainly what we are seeing. The hands are enormous, but have you noticed that we cannot see any more of his left arm; the hand has hidden the rest.

We've talked before about drawing what you see. Well you can see that the light source is behind him because his hands are in shadow but his right arm is not. We see his right arm in full and his left leg. Part of his head shows through his fingers, and his right foot and ankle.

You could try making similar contorted shapes in the mirror. Notice how different parts of the body appear as you move them back and forth.

Mounting your drawing

There are two basic reasons why you might want to mount your artwork – one for protection, and another – because you're proud of it!

A mount is a cardboard frame that will stop your drawing from becoming torn at the edges. You can buy pre-cut mounts or cut your own from a sheet of card.

How you present your drawing is something else you might want to consider. Look at the drawing of the woman opposite. Part of her head is actually covered by the frame, and that was the artist's choice. It looks good and maybe looked just a bit too ordinary to mount it with her whole head in the frame.

The drawing below is a landscape scene – maybe this was part of a larger drawing.

What next?

The aim of this book was to show you a variety of techniques that will enable you to enjoy drawing. We've also looked at a variety of different types of drawing, such as still life, the living world, landscape and figure drawing.

If on the way through this book, you feel you've gained confidence and have managed to express yourself through your drawing, then that is excellent.

So what comes next?

Add colour to your drawing. Why not venture into other forms of media?

Well there's other dry media – now that you've had practice using pencil you're definitely ready to move on to coloured pencils, and then charcoal and pastels.

Look at the page opposite. These are pencil crayons at the top – you can also use watercolour pencils and you'll find some pencil drawings in the following pages. The centrepiece is a wonderful box of pastels and you'll be able see some pastel work also.

There are also charcoal sticks. Charcoal has probably been used as a drawing tool since the invention of fire. It's wonderfully adaptable (and smudging can be intentional as well as accidental) and can be used with other media such as pen and ink or pastels.

Pen, ink, and watercolour, known as wet media – are frequently used together.

Why not read on and see exactly what you could do?

Pen and ink

Drawing with pen and ink gives a very precise line, as you can see from the drawings on these two pages. The drawing above shows fine parallel lines filling an area and this gives us the illusion of tone. The weight of the line (thickness of pen nib) can make the drawing darker or lighter.

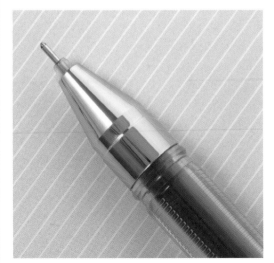

Pen and ink can work well with a more relaxed approach – foliage is a great example. In Western art, pen and ink work can be traced back to the monks of the ninth century, which decorated their manuscripts.

The possibilities and varieties of expression are limitless and this medium can, as you read at the beginning of this section, be used with other media, in particular watercolour.

The best method of creating tone and texture in ink drawing is with hatching. The closer the lines are together the darker the tone appears, and there is less white paper showing. A thicker pen also gives a darker appearance.

Of course you can use cross-hatching and all of the other techniques we have looked at with pencil. Pen and ink drawing gives a very crisp or delicate finish if you're using a fine pen.

Your choice of pen will depend upon your style of drawing and personal taste. You could use a drafting pen but if you do, then buy ink made for that pen, otherwise it might become blocked.

You can buy bottles of Indian ink and use dipping pens or fountain pens. Some artists even use the common biro, but remember the ink is not permanent. Popular pens these days include the rollerball – they're quite inexpensive and very comfortable to use.

Coloured pencils

Most of us have probably used coloured pencils – they always arrived at birthdays with a 'colouring in' book.

Now we can buy watercolour pencils, which can be used wet or dry. They look the same but are much easier to use and give a better finish.

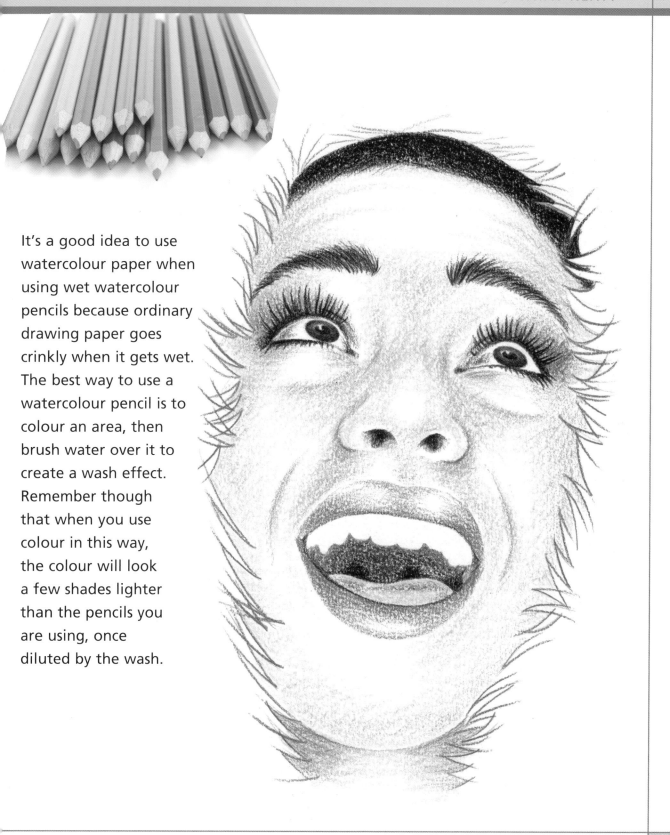

It's a good idea to use watercolour paper when using wet watercolour pencils because ordinary drawing paper goes crinkly when it gets wet. The best way to use a watercolour pencil is to colour an area, then brush water over it to create a wash effect. Remember though that when you use colour in this way, the colour will look a few shades lighter than the pencils you are using, once diluted by the wash.

Charcoal

Charcoal is a medium which people either love or hate. It's a medium which goes a step further than pencil in that it can instantly create a wonderful rich black that is impossible with the pencil. But there is a downside. Charcoal can be very messy and if you choose to work with charcoal you'll find it on your hands and your sleeves and, far more serious, you'll have left finger marks all over your paper.

As soon as you finish your painting you must fix it with a fixative spray. As with pastels,
if you don't fix your finished charcoal study
it will smudge.

You can use any type of paper such as pastel paper or watercolour paper and you'll find that some art suppliers sell pads of charcoal paper, which has a texture that holds the charcoal. You can also use heavy quality cartridge paper. You might like the idea
of using tinted papers.

You'll find, as you become practised with using charcoal, that you find ways of making your charcoal work for you. You're not stuck with using a charcoal stick which draws only thick lines – you can sharpen your charcoal stick – try rubbing it gently on a piece of sandpaper. It certainly helps when drawing facial details which can, of course, be very fiddly. You'll need to keep on sharpening your point – it doesn't last long.

Pastels

If you think pastel drawing means drawing in pale colours you are wrong, but you are not alone. A pastel stick isn't a high grade chalk, pastel is made from pigment that is ground into a paste and then a gum binder is added. The word pastel actually comes from the French word 'pastiche'. It's a very crumbly stick and you need to be careful to avoid smudging your paper. For many beginners pastels are easy to use. They're available in many colours (including very vivid ones). When you've finished your work you should use a fixative spray that will stop smudging. You can buy a fixative spray from art shops.

There are many types of papers that are produced for pastel work, and to a certain extent the type of paper you use will depend on whether you are using hard pastels or soft pastels. Soft pastels are probably easier to begin with. However, use a heavy cartridge paper for practising and if you find that pastels are a medium that you like then you can start to experiment with other papers. Pastel paper is available in many colours and textures that can enhance the appearance of your work.

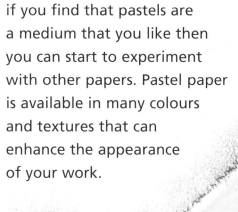

Watercolour painting

If you feel inclined to take up watercolour painting you'll need paints, brushes, something to keep your water in, a mixing palette, a board, a pencil, watercolour paper and a putty rubber.

Watercolour paints are available in either pats of colour or in tubes. Tubes are convenient when painting large areas, as you don't need to keep going back to the pat to refill your brush. They're also cleaner as you don't have a problem with getting the colours mixed. Pats, however, are easier if you want to paint out of doors.

There are a wide variety of brushes that you can choose from. The difference between the brushes, apart from size, is cost, the amount of water they hold and what effects can be created with them.

If you haven't done any painting before (or at least not since you were in school) then you could simply choose just a few different types, but make sure they're watercolour brushes. Eventually you'll be able to be more discriminating in your choice. Most brushes are made in synthetic materials now, and they are cheaper than the non-synthetic varieties.

One item that is useful to have is a travel set. It folds up very small and has room for a small brush and also has a water container, you have to fill a section in the lid but when you're ready to paint you pour the water into the container. Then at the end you just tip the water away and pack up.